FAMILY Reformation

FAMILY Reformation

THE LEGACY *of* SOLA SCRIPTURA *in* CALVIN'S GENEVA

BY: SCOTT BROWN

MERCHANT ADVENTURERS
WAKE FOREST, NORTH CAROLINA

Other Books by Scott Brown

A Church in the House
Restoring Daily Worship to the Christian Household

How does a father lead his family as a shepherd of his household? In this sermon, Matthew Henry explains how fathers can fulfill divine commands for fathers in their family life. Edited by Scott Brown.

Feminine by Design
The Twelve Pillars of Biblical Womanhood

How does a young girl learn what it means to be a woman? The world needs Christ-loving, husband-helping, home-making, dominion-taking, kingdom-advancing women. The "Twelve Pillars" show the way.

Helping Them to Choose
The Duty of Parents

What should parents do to help their children choose a marriage partner? This guidebook from 1859 gives helpful instruction for coaching your children on their way to the marriage altar. Edited by Scott Brown.

First Printing: June 2009

Merchant Adventurers, Inc.

3721 Quarry Rd Wake Forest, North Carolina 27587

www.NCFIC.org

ISBN-10: 0-9820567-5-3
ISBN-13: 978-0-9820567-5-2

Cover Design By Justin Turley
Book Design By David Edward Brown

PRINTED IN THE UNITED STATES OF AMERICA

NAVIGATION

TABLE OF CONTENTS

The Gold Standard for Family Life. The Family Was Being Reformed.
Dealing with Crisis, Then and Now. A Case Study for Exposing and
Challenging the Idols of the Day. The Victories of the Sixteenth Century
- and Ours. The Price of Family Reformation. General Reformations
Fall Short Without Family Reformation. Family Reformation Spreads
to America. We Are the Beneficiaries of Calvin's Family Reformation.
The Calvinistic Seeds of Family Reformation Are Still Sprouting.

CHAPTER 2
THE INSIDE STORY

Depriving Asses of Their Lion's Skin. A House of Inventions. The
Church Deluded. Errors, Lies, Frauds and Iniquities. Inventions in
the Church. Thralldom. As Goes the Church, So Goes the Family.

SECTION II. CALVIN SPEAKS

CHAPTER 6
THE FAMILY AS A FOUNDATION

Mercy To Thousands. Consolation in Times of Trouble: God's Mercy is Extended from Fathers To Their Children's Children. Visiting the Iniquity of the Fathers upon the Children. Visiting the Sins of the Fathers upon Following Generations.

CHAPTER 7
THE SWEETNESS OF MARRIAGE

God - the Author and Patron of Marriage. Not Profitable to Be Alone. What Does It Mean to Leave and Cleave? The Two Shall Become One. Two Under One Name. Marriage a Covenant - United by God's Authority. The Divine Good in the Order of Marriage. Obligations of Marriage. The Dignity of Marriage. Christ's High View of Marriage. The Example of the Apostles in Mixing Ministry and Marriage. Prohibition of Marriage - an Idea for Heretics. Calvin's Attack of Catholic Law on Marriage. Against the Oath of Celibacy. Doctrines of Devils for Marriage.

CHAPTER 8
THE "STRONG AFFECTION" OF A HUSBAND

What Kind of Love Must a Husband Give? One Flesh - Loving and Hating Your Own Body. Who Is "The Savior of the Body"? Male Headship Explained. A Husband's Headship Resembles Christ's. A

Husband's Protection of His Wife. The Man is a Monster Who Does Not Love His Wife. The Danger of Tyranny in Marriage. Degrees of Union - Marriage More Sacred Than Other Relationships.

CHAPTER 9
A WIFE, THE DISTINGUISHED ORNAMENT OF MAN

The Woman Is a Distinguished Ornament of the Man.   Eve - The Inseparable Associate of Adam's Life. A Wife - The Man's Consort and Companion.   "The Best Companion of My Life" - Written Upon the Death of Calvin's Wife. A Companion and Associate for the Sweetest Harmony in Marriage.   The Various Yokes of Submission.   Thy Desire Shall Be Unto Thy Husband.   Advice To a Young Woman for Her Marriage.   Encouragement for a Wife.   Advice To a Wife Whose Husband Was Captured.   For Wives with Unbelieving Husbands. Letter To a Wife with an Unbelieving Husband.   Mutual Obligations for Authority and Submission.

CHAPTER 10
THE PRESERVATION OF MARRIAGE

The Common Sense of Mankind Declares Adultery to Be Obscene. God Loves Chastity and Purity. Understanding Adultery of the Heart-How to Avoid Being Dull and Stupid in Judging Our Sins. The Heart of Adultery. The Eyes Are As Torches to Inflame the Heart to Lust. A Severe Warning To Adulterers.   Bridle All Lusts.   Wrong Done To a Young Wife. The Slippery Slope of Lust While Young. Why Divorce Is Repugnant and Abolishes What God Has Joined Together.   How Wives Are "Miserably Tormented."   Christ on Divorce - Tearing the Body in Pieces. Impious Divorce Brings Just Punishment. Polygamy is Perverse and Degenerate.

CHAPTER 11

THE BLESSING OF CHILDREN

Children Are a Treasure. Celebrating the Kindness of God in Giving Offspring. Polluting Children with Religious Superstitions. Children: Heritage and Reward. Through Children Men Are Defended. How Children Shut the Mouths of the Malevolent. In Praise of Fertility. Childbearing - a Heroic Virtue.

CHAPTER 12

THE SALVATION OF CHILDREN

Corruption of Sin Passed on To Children. Children - Born Defiled by Sin's Stains.

CHAPTER 13

THE FATHER'S DISCIPLESHIP OF CHILDREN

Fathers and Children Restored from Discord To Unity. Advice for a Parent on the Greatest Benefit That Can Be Granted To Children. A Fatherhood That Transmits Doctrine To Children. Fathers - Diligent and Assiduous in Teaching Their Children. The Knowledge of God Published from Age To Age Without Interruption.

CHAPTER 14

CATECHIZING CHILDREN

The Importance of Catechisms for Children. Catechizing Children - To Arouse Slothful Parents.

CHAPTER 15

The Discipline of Children

Severity of Correction for Children Required. Unreasonable Severity or Kind Liberal Treatment. The Heart of a Parent - Drawing Nearer To Christ.

CHAPTER 16

How Parents Respond to Prodigals

The Exuberance of Paternal Kindness. The Compassion of a Father.

CHAPTER 17

Honor and Obedience Toward Parents

Despising Father Is Despising God. Obedience of Children Enforced By the Authority of God. Submission - a Step in Our Ascent To the Supreme Parent. Children to Be Obedient in All Things - What Does "All" Mean? Long Life - a Gift of God in This Present Life. Forbidden: Detracting From the Dignity of Father and Mother. Those Who Violate Parental Authority Are Monsters. Curses for Disobedient Children. Punishment for Striking Father and Mother. How to Respond To Parents Who Are Too Harsh.

CHAPTER 18

The Marriages of Children

The Dangers and Advantages of Singleness. Is It Best to Be Married or Single? The Common Duty of Parents. Unequally Yoked. On Marrying Idolaters. They Have Polluted Holiness and Married Foreign Wives. Marrying for the Sake of Beauty. Choosing a Wife for the Elegance of Her Form. Marriage Is Too Sacred for the Lust of the Eyes. Intermarrying in Families. Why Did He Refuse an Opportunity for Marriage? A Daughter's Willing Consent. Breaking Marriage Engagements. The Seriousness of Betrothal. Fathers Held Responsible for Proofs of Virginity. Children Getting Married. Children Who Commit To Marriage Without Parental Consent. Old Men Marrying Younger Women. A Coerced Vow to Marry Made Null.

CHAPTER 19
The Family at Church

Relating With Spiritual Fathers - Don't Spare or Indulge. Gentleness with Brothers in the Church. The Marriage of an Elder. The Children of an Elder. Ruling a Family Trains and Adapts a Man for Ruling a Church. Women Speaking in a "Duly Regulated Assembly." What Does the Law Have to Do with Women Speaking in Church? When Can Women Teach? Older Women Keeping Younger Women from Imprudence.

CHAPTER 20
Modesty

The Spiritual Adorning of the Soul. Women's Clothing That Does Not "Hit the Golden Mean." On Extravagance - the Servant's Gifts of Ornaments To Rebekah.

Remember the Realities of Our Sanctification. Remember the Humanity of All Men. Remember the Flaws of Our Fathers in the Faith. Remember to Ask Calvin's Question.

SECTION IV. The Rest of the Story

CHAPTER 25
An Effective Family Reformation

What About a Family Reformation Today?

CHAPTER 26
Twelve Signs of Today's Family Reformation

1. Revival of Biblical Fatherhood. 2. Large Families. 3. Rejection of Feminism. 4. Modest Dress. 5. Early Manhood. 6. Persecution. 7. Generational Retention. 8. Books on Family Life. 9. Resurgence of Expository Preaching. 10. Clarification of the Gospel. 11. Doctrinal Awareness. 12. Family Integrated Church Movement.

CHAPTER 27
Hope for the Future

DEDICATION

This book is dedicated to those who worked like beavers to get this book out in time for Calvin's 500th birthday including my wife Deborah; my children Blair, David, and Claudia; Peter and Kelly Bradrick; my parents Bill and Mary Brown; Monica Daming; and last, but not least, the Spring 2009 Interns of *The National Center for Family-Integrated Churches*: Micah Ferrill, Joseph Froemming, Andrew Gillingham, Ryan Glick, and Andrew Higginbotham.

"MY HEART I OFFER TO YOU, O LORD,
PROMPTLY AND SINCERELY."

- John Calvin

INTRODUCTION

While the doctrine of salvation was being reformed during the sixteenth century, so were marriage, manhood, womanhood, fatherhood, motherhood, courtship, child raising, fertility, and almost every area that touches family life.

John Calvin never wrote a book on the family, but he touched off a family reformation. God appointed him to be the instigator of a massive restructuring of the most fundamental institution of society – the family.

The Reformer of Geneva was a repository of scriptural wisdom on law, politics, economics, and dozens of areas of practical Christian living. God blessed him with the ability to understand and apply the Word of God in a way that few men have ever equaled. Calvin's instruction on the family was not only extensive in sheer quantity, but also comprehensive in its scope, speaking to almost every area of the family.

Like no other reformer, Calvin provided the exegetical precision that defined the terms for a biblical vision of family life.

With crystal clarity he explained the details of how the family had exchanged the truth of God for a lie.

We should remember and give thanks for this dear brother for excavating the gold mines of the Bible and exposing the raw biblical language and bedrock principles that form the doctrine of the Christian family. This book seeks to communicate the main themes of Calvin's teaching on family life in his own words, using quotes from his books, sermons, letters, and other writings.

It is striking to notice the simple means that God used to generate this family reformation. It was doctrinally oriented and arose from the rich soil of a vision of the majesty of God, a belief in the perfection and sufficiency of Scripture, a practical and tenderhearted pastoral care, a devotion to expository preaching, and the real transformation of those who were reforming their lives to this biblical teaching.

The family reformation in Geneva needs to be understood in the twenty-first century because it sets before us a biblical vision for family life and reminds us of the upheaval that accompanies public family reformation.

Section I

Anatomy of a Family Reformation

CHAPTER 1

WHY IS CALVIN'S FAMILY REFORMATION IMPORTANT TODAY?

A Case Study for Family Reformation Today

How can a pastor from five hundred years ago have anything to say about modern family issues? Isn't Calvin so vastly disconnected with our times as to render him completely irrelevant in finding answers to modern issues? On the contrary, the controlling principle of Calvin's teaching 500 years ago is indispensible to help you reform your family life according to Scripture in the 21st century.

This book proposes that the application of the Reformation understanding of Scripture - *sola Scriptura* - inescapably transforms family life. Geneva was the cradle of the reformation of Christian family culture and it illustrates both how to reform the family and how the reformed family may impact society.

The Gold Standard for Family Life

The scriptural wisdom which Calvin applied in Geneva is the same wisdom which we need to reform the family in our generation, for the sufficiency of Scripture is the gold standard for family life. This principle can launch a family reformation today, just as it did in Geneva.

The cry of *"sola Scriptura"* is necessary if we ever hope to escape the bondage of our family killing culture. We can learn much from the Genevan reformation because it was a revival of doctrine applied to every area of life, resulting in practices that were consistent with those principles. Real families were rescued and real families prevailed.

The Family Was Being Reformed

When you say the words "Protestant Reformation," most people immediately think of Luther, Calvin, justification by faith, and the *"five Solas."* Of course, they are right to think of these things for they were central components of the Reformation. But to limit it to those few people and ideas is to woefully misunderstand the breadth and scope of the Reformation. Calvin's Geneva experienced a reformation of all of life. No area of life escaped the scrutiny of the Reformers. The doctrine of salvation was one of many areas being reformed - the family was another. In fact, the reforms of family life were extremely visible and controversial in churches and homes of that time.

Family issues consumed much of the schedule of the Consistory* in Geneva, with "roughly 60% of the Consistory's entire case load was devoted to issues of sex, marriage, and family." [1] It was a time of family reformation.

Dealing with Crisis, Then and Now

When you read the registers of the Consistory, and Calvin's commentaries, letters, and sermons, it quickly becomes apparent that the battles of the sixteenth century family were similar to the battles facing the family today. The modern family is in collapse, much like the family collapse that John Calvin dealt with among his flock. But at that dark time for the family, the light of Scripture dawned, shining into a world that had forgotten what God said about family life. As a result, a revived vision of God and His Word spread blessing and healing on the land, transforming both heart and hearth. The church was in desperate need of doctrinal and practical reforms in family life then, as the church is now. Today the vestiges of biblical family life are being extinguished from

---

* "In order to establish... discipline [and] to promote... Christian manner of living, each Reformed community tried to establish institutions to oversee the mores of all members of the community... The Consistory was established as a new tribunal, with about twenty-five members: twelve elders, elected each year, and, ex-officio, all the pastors of the city." [2]

modern churches and families, and most people don't even know it. Comparing our time with their's reveals many insights not only on how the family departs from the biblical pattern but also how it can make its way back.

A Case Study for Exposing and Challenging the Idols of the Day

The family reformation in Geneva teaches us many lessons about gospel ministry. The proper application of the gospel includes discerning and casting down the idols that grip the culture. Many of the battles for the family in Geneva were over the propositions of idols amassed in Satan's war with the "seed of the woman." Lessons from these kinds of conflicts are put before us in Geneva, teaching us how we should respond to the twenty-first century idol's being propogated by Hollywood, Washington, Wall Street, and the gods of established "Religion."

The Victories of the Sixteenth Century - and Ours

There were many victories in Geneva for the battle to reform the family. It is important to look at these victories because they help us define what a return to Scripture looks like. In this book, we chronicle many of these examples with the hope that it will help us visualize what we need to accomplish in our own day.

To win the battles of the collapse of the twenty-first century family, it is helpful to understand the victories of the sixteenth century. There were multitudes of such victories. It is a historically documented reality that the Reformers experienced a revival of biblical womanhood, an attention to the details of Scripture on dozens of practical family matters, an unusual turning of fathers' hearts to their children, a revival of love and biblical purpose in marriage, a recovery of the disciplines of family life in the form of catechisms and what we call "family worship," a restructuring of premarital practices for courtship and betrothal and even the wedding day, and an overall elevation of the importance of family life. Calvin initiated a paradigm shift of thinking on family life. He called family relationships sacred in a culture that exalted singleness and childlessness.

By identifying the victories of the sixteenth century, let us raise a standard and clarify our own vision of victory in the twenty-first century.

The Price of Family Reformation

The family reformation in Geneva is important to us because it reminds us of the difficulties that accompany the public reformation of family life. The reformations in family life led to persecution. However, because the old adage is true - "The blood of the martyrs is the seed of the church" - the persecutions only intensified and proliferated the changes brought on by the Reformation.

General Reformations Fall Short
Without Family Reformation

What does Calvin's Reformation in Geneva teach us about reformations in general? Perhaps one of the great lessons of the Protestant Reformation is this: reformations that do not stand on the broad applications of the sufficiency of Scripture will quickly fall away and have little impact on future generations.

Calvin seemed to have a vivid consciousness of fathers passing on their faith to the next generation. Fathers were challenged to teach their children so that "when we are dead, a holy course of living may survive and remain."[3]

Calvin advocated that the faith of the fathers should be passed on to the next generation. Biblical thinking, which includes multigenerational intentionality on family life was ignited in Geneva and we still see its effects today. Although there were many failures in future generations after Calvin, the reformation in Geneva had an unmistakable multigenerational orientation.

When it comes to revivals, we often see that they are a flash in the pan which does not continue on into the next generation. One reason this happens is because there was not a corresponding family reformation. If the focus is only on one doctrine - the doctrine of salvation for example - but ignores the whole counsel of God, the reformation may die with the reformers. If fathers neglect the commands of God regarding family life and do not teach their children, their reformation may end with them (Judges 2:10-13).

A revival movement which ignores the commands and practices of biblical family life and expands at the expense of children, marriages, and biblical family life cannot stand beyond its own time. Not only does it expire under the weight of the judgment of God for despising major categories of Scripture regarding family relationships, it does not have the multigenerational mentality it needs to pass the reformation on to upcoming generations.

Family Reformation Spreads to America

As the doctrine of the Reformers came to America in the seventeenth century, Calvin's understanding of the family was applied by families in the early settlements. As years passed in America, these principles were compromised as a result of rising worldly philosophies and Enlightenment thought, resulting in common attacks against the doctrine of *sola Scriptura*. But, even though there was a waning of biblical principles of family life, we see its flames fanned again during the Great Awakening. Great Awakening preachers like George Whitefield, Jonathan Edwards, and Samuel Davies, men who had their roots in the family reformation of Geneva many years before, delivered sermons and wrote tracts promoting biblical family life. In the same way that family reforms were activated in Geneva, fathers in America were challenged, marriages were reordered, attention was given to the rising generation through family worship, and children were brought under the government of God. As a result, one aspect of the first Great Awakening was a fresh awakening in family life. This occurred because the great preachers of the Great Awakening were aware of the legacy of the Reformers and their Puritan forefathers on these matters.

We Are the Beneficiaries of Calvin's Family Reformation

To a degree, we in America are beneficiaries of Geneva's reforms. Our founding fathers promoted Calvin's vision of family life, greatly affecting the prosperity of our nation. However, at the same time, we must acknowledge the broad trends in our culture which make it clear that we now despise the things which led to the family reformations of the past.

In the twenty-first century, the mainstream evangelical church has despised marriage by dismantling its purpose, the husband's authority, and the wife's submission to her husband. It has exalted singleness and the family-free life. It has re-defined marriage to include homosexual unions. It has banished children from the discipleship of adults in the church. It has accepted the child-banning philosophy of birth control as normal. It has endorsed handing children over to God-hating mentors in government education. It has facilitated age segregation which contradicts Scripture and defeats church and family discipleship. It has embraced divorce as a normal course. It has promoted the dishonor of the elderly by putting them in sterile, institutional, state-controlled, euthanasia-friendly environments without the care of family. Amazingly, Calvin spoke to many of these family issues.

The Calvinistic Seeds of Family Reformation Are Still Sprouting

Five hundred years after Calvin's birth, the seeds of family reformation are still being planted and families are still being reformed according to the principle of *sola Scriptura*. In America today, there is a family reformation movement afoot which is based on the same basic principle as the family reformation of Geneva. Because of a revival of Calvinistic theology and the emphasis on *Sola Scriptura*, families are rediscovering what the Bible says about manhood and womanhood, marriage, family worship, the blessing of children, birth control, modesty, the naming of children, and the hearts of fathers turning toward children. Let me also suggest that the modern homeschool movement is a result of the resuscitation of Calvin's principles inspiring biblical thinking on education. Those who say they homeschool because God has commanded education by parents "when you sit in your house, when you walk by the way, when you lie down and when you rise up" (Deuteronomy 8:9) are thinking biblically about. Homeschooling gained traction among Christians in America because they dared to believe that the Bible had something to say about education.

Thus the foundational principle – sola Scriptura - of the family reformation which began almost five hundred years ago is still alive in families today who are being reformed by looking toward Scripture alone as the basis for their practices.

CHAPTER 2

THE INSIDE STORY

The Dark Underbelly of Family Life

C alvin exposed the dark underbelly of family life created by the religious systems of sixteenth century Europe. He did this deliberately with the exactitude of a brain surgeon. As he faithfully exposited Scripture, he saw how far families had drifted from the commands of God.

Depriving Asses of Their Lion's Skin

He resolutely declared his intention to reform the family. When speaking of his attempt to reveal the falsehoods of Catholicism concerning marriage, he said, "Much has been gained, if I have, in some measure, deprived these asses of their lion's skin."[1] When speaking of reforming baptism practices, he said that we must "omit from baptism all theatrical pomp, which dazzles the eyes of the simple and deadens their minds."[2]

A House of Inventions

The sixteenth century family was a house of human inventions. As a result, the basic functions of family life had been conformed to cultural norms and extra-biblical religious principles. In many ways, it was a house of horrors. A quarter of the population had taken vows of celibacy; a utilitarian philosophy of marriage had dampened love; destructive premarital practices compromised the purity of the younger generation; women were deprived of marriage and motherhood in sterile institutional life; fathers neglected their family shepherding responsibilities; church discipline was absent even in the face of adultery. Family life was on the rocks.

Families in John Calvin's Geneva were suffering as a result of the departures they had made from the biblical pattern of family life. Sound familiar? The problems of family life in Calvin's Geneva were hauntingly like our own, reminding us of the modern-day collapse of the family and biblical family life in the twenty-first century. Departures from the Word of God, being the inventions of man, always have their downside, for God offers "curses" for those who disobey (Deuteronomy 27:11-26).

Calvin's teaching on the family was immediately practical and struck at the heart of contemporary issues. He put his finger in the wounds of family life and the medicine he applied was the water of life - the Word of God. He addressed the family problems of his day with Scripture alone.

The Church Deluded

Calvin was clear that family life needed many reforms. He believed the church was severely deluded in many areas related to the family.

Sometimes we are tempted to look back at history and see "the good ol' days." We often think that the days of old were better than our day. This may be true in certain eras, but Calvin would not have us think of the sixteenth century as the "good ol' days." Far from seeing his times as some nostalgic era to look back to and emulate, Calvin believed the family of his day to be severely off course. He blamed the problem on the religious leaders and the unbiblical system they created.

Errors, Lies, Frauds and Iniquities

While the Roman Catholic Church had all the trappings of success, in reality it was fraudulently misrepresenting the teaching of Scripture. It had the cash flow, the applause of the people, and popular tradition, but it lacked the moral authority of Scripture. Calvin unleashed verbal fury on the way that the Roman Church had harmed the first relationship of family life - marriage. Calvin sought to expose the false philosophies and practices of the Roman system and reveal that the Catholic lion was not a lion at all. Calvin used devastating language to expose the reality of its game. He wrote,

And, that they might not delude the Church in this matter merely, what a long series of errors, lies, frauds, and iniquities have they appended to one error? So that you may say they sought nothing but a hiding-place for abominations when they converted marriage into a sacrament. When once they obtained this, they appropriated to themselves the cognizance of conjugal causes: as the thing was spiritual, it was not to be intermeddled with by profane judges. Then they enacted laws by which they confirmed their tyranny, - laws partly impious toward God, partly fraught with injustice toward men; such as, that marriages contracted between minors, without the consent of their parents, should be valid; that no lawful marriages can be contracted between relations within the seventh degree, and that such marriages, if contracted, should be dissolved. Moreover, they frame degrees of kindred contrary to the laws of all nations, and even the polity of Moses, and enact that a husband who has repudiated an adulteress may not marry again - that spiritual kindred cannot be joined in marriage - that marriage cannot be celebrated from Septuagesimo to the Octaves of Easter, three weeks before the nativity of John, nor from Advent to Epiphany, and innumerable others, which it were too tedious to mention. We must now get out of their mire, in which our discourse has stuck longer than our inclination. Methinks, however, that much has been gained if I have, in some measure, deprived these asses of their lion's skin.[3]

The cloistered life of the sixteenth century promoted rampant immorality among the priests and the monks - perhaps in the same way that prolonged singleness does today.

Femininity and motherhood were stolen from women and they were isolated in sterile, childless, family-free environments - perhaps in the same way that feminism has degraded motherhood and children today.

Marriage had become the second-class, less-desirable choice while celibacy was honored - perhaps in the same way that marriage is delayed for fun and games today.

Adultery and abuse by men was accepted with no recourse for women thus treated - perhaps in the same way that women are dishonored by unfaithful husbands with no discipline from the church today.

Premarital sex was rampant and purity before marriage ended with the lift of a glass and a promise of marriage - perhaps in the same way that premarital sex is rampant among engaged couples today.

Courtship practices caused defrauding by allowing false promises and by participating in systems that trivialized marriage and everything leading up to it - perhaps in the same way that the "dating" culture has promoted one "mini-divorce" after another today.

Children were being named after idols or "saints" - perhaps the same way that parents disregard the biblical understanding of names and name their children for the sound of a name or after celebrities and athletes today.

Due to the man-made inventions that flourished and choked the life out of the family, it was a bad time for marriages, families, women, and children - perhaps in the same way that it is today, with families struggling to survive in a depraved culture.

Inventions in the Church

These inventions of family life conformed to similar unbiblical inventions in the Church. The same philosophy that caused the Church to reinvent itself, was adopted by the family. The Roman church had added hundreds of "inventions" to its practice, and the family adopted the same philosophy. Calvin states,

> Nor do we do this as those miserable men who habitually bind over their minds to the thralldom of superstition; but we feel that the undoubted power of his divine majesty lives and breathes there [in Scripture].
>
> The two great pillars upon which the kingdom of Satan is erected, and by which it is upheld, are ignorance and error; the first step of our mission from this spiritual thralldom consists in having our eyes opened, and being turned from darkness to light, Acts xxvi. 18. "However, we do not depend on the wisdom of man, nor upon our own reason to know the truth. We rest wholly upon the Word of God, written, and upon the work of the Holy

*Spirit. For the Scriptures alone give all the glory to God;
by their light and power to convince and convert sinners,
to comfort and build up believers unto salvation: but the
Spirit of God bearing witness by and with the scriptures
in the heart of man, is alone able fully to persuade it that
they are the very word of God.*[4]

Thralldom

Thralldom is a disposition of servitude or submission or a state of
complete absorption in things unbiblical. The Roman Church had
become "Thralldom Central," with the popes adding one thing
after another to keep the people and the money coming. Calvin
attacked these thralldoms of the Roman church and appealed for
a return to Scripture. John Knox also assailed them saying, "All
worshipping, honouring, or service invented by the brain of man
in the religion of God, without his own express commandment,
is idolatry. The Mass is invented by the brain of man, without any
commandment of God; therefore it is idolatry."[5]

The leaders of the Catholic Church knew what modern mega-
churches understand: if you can enrapture and thrill the people,
they will become addicted to your inventions and keep coming
back. Like modern evangelicalism, the Roman Church created
itself as it went along and whatever worked was practiced, whether
it was candles for worship, infant exorcisms at baptism, or complex
and costly "programs" (such as pilgrimages).

The reformers would have nothing of this, so out went the litany (prayers to the saints), pilgrimages, benefices, indulgences, sacerdotalism, altars, kneeling at communion, auricular confession, the cult of Mary and the saints, the celebration of holy days and feast days, prayers for the dead, pictures of Christ, icons and crosses. Out went the belief in purgatory, the sign of the cross, crucifixes, images and elaborate ritual, surplices (or choir dress) and Eucharistic vestments. Out went popes, bishops, archbishops, monks, friars, canons regular, cathedral dignitaries, archdeacons, rural deans, canon lawyers, prebendaries, chaplains. Out went hierarchical titles from archbishop to acolyte of the archbishop, the "tonsure" (the monk's haircut), the obligation of clerical celibacy, clerical dress, clerical estate, clerical lifestyles, and clerical privilege (including immunity from the secular courts).

With the Reformation came a simple service based on preaching and Bible study. Prayers and the Psalms were sung to popular tunes. The people, formerly passive spectators, became active participants. They were encouraged to sing God's praise with all their hearts. They were seated corporately at the communion table, to receive both wine and bread.

In came biblical church government. Elders and deacons were appointed to handle church affairs. Congregations gave consent for hiring and firing of ministers. There was softening of the clergy/laity distinction. There were "ministers" rather than "priests." With a stroke they challenged the whole system.

Consider the need for reformation in our time and the addictive thralldoms we have created in order to thrill the people in the meetings of the church with practices that have no command, principle, or pattern in Scripture.

As Goes the Church, So Goes the Family

The same spirit of invention that overcame the church also overcame the family. When the church departs from Scripture, the family is not far behind. And when the family departs from Scripture, the culture is not far behind. If the three spheres of human society (the church, the family, and the state) are houses of inventions, chaos reigns and the glory of the Lord departs.

Church and family life are remarkably intertwined. When the churches go astray, whole families go with them - often, for many generations.

CHAPTER 3

SEVEN POWERFUL IGNITERS

The Flint and Steel of Family Reformation

W herever the flames of awakening have burned, there were key igniters which discharged to cause it. What were the great igniters that caused such a tremendous shift in the view of the family in Calvin's day? Once activated, what fueled the fires of the family reformation in Geneva? There were at least seven factors that promoted the reformation of the family. First, there was a doctrinal foundation - the sufficiency of Scripture. Second, there was a pulpit practice - expository preaching. Third, there was the exposure of controversial revolutionary texts of Scripture - powerful texts. Fourth, there was a way of thinking that facilitated the reforms - doctrinal precision. Fifth, there was an unusual perspective - a high view of the family. Sixth, there was an outpouring of practical tools, literally a surge of written resources for the family. Seventh, there were visible examples to follow - tangible reforms in real families. These seven factors sped the family reformation on its way.

1. Doctrinal Foundation - *Sola Scriptura*

Reformations are wonderful gifts of God because they refresh in a way that is only possible through a return to the Word of God. They are fundamentally about transforming our beliefs and practices to the patterns of the Scriptures. At the heart of true reformations is a renewed obedience to the command of Christ delivered in the Great Commission: "Go ye therefore, and teach all nations...to observe all things whatsoever I have commanded you" (Matthew 28:19-20).

The doctrinal foundation from which the family reformation was launched was the doctrine of the sufficiency of Scripture. This was the primary cause of the reformation. This doctrine, known in the Reformation as *sola Scriptura*, teaches that Scripture is sufficient to instruct us in all areas of life and godliness.

Calvin's strict adherence to the Scriptures was the genius of the Reformation in Geneva. Instead of thinking that the Bible was only adequate for certain circumstances, Calvin regarded it as the supreme reference point for all situations. Calvin believed that the Bible contained all that was necessary for life and godliness, and as a result, the whole of Scripture was scanned for answers to every question and for solutions to every problem. The battle cry of the reformers was *"sola Scriptura"* or "Scripture Alone!" This meant that they dealt with difficult texts and did not skirt their clear meanings for the sake of their traditions.

Holding the Bible to be the only reliable sourcebook for the answers to family questions, Calvin was relentless in removing anything in family life that did not find a pattern or command in Scripture, and embracing all which did. He believed that "All Scripture is given by inspiration of God, and is profitable for doctrine, for reproof, for correction, for instruction in righteousness" (2 Timothy 3:16).

Embracing the doctrine of the sufficiency of Scripture is critical for us to understand how to reform the family.

2. Pulpit Practice - Expository Preaching

Calvin was first and foremost an expositor and pastor. As a good expositor, he dealt with the issues that were in the text of Scripture, and when "family" was in the text, he did not avoid it. Instead, he waxed eloquent and spoke fearlessly. Like every good pastor, he applied Scripture to everything, including the family. This faithful expository method mixed with a heart for pastoral care sparked a family reformation.

Calvin insisted that Christians needed to be limited within the boundaries of Scripture because of the perfection of Christ's teaching. He said,

> *The Church has been given the perfection of Christ's teaching. With this we should be content and learn not to invent anything new for ourselves or take over anything invented by others. It is all summed up in the words*

> *spoken from heaven by God at the Transfiguration: 'This*
> *is my beloved son; hear him' (Matt. 17:5).*[1]

For every area of life, there was no other legitimate mode of teaching.

> *Let this, then, be the firm principle, that nothing else is*
> *to be regarded as the Word of God and given a place in*
> *the Church than what is contained first in the Law and*
> *the Prophets and then in the Apostles' writings; and that*
> *there is no other mode of teaching aright in the Church*
> *except by the prescript and norm of God's Word.*[2]

As he expounded on the doctrine of God, Calvin offered many warnings against making a god in our own image and to our own liking. He says,

> *Therefore, let us willingly remain hedged in by those*
> *boundaries within which God has been pleased to confine*
> *our persons, and as it were, enclose our minds, so as to*
> *prevent them from losing themselves by wandering*
> *unrestrained.*[3]

The family reformation in Geneva happened because of faithful exposition of Scripture. If we ever hope to reform the family in our generation, that same devotion to exposition will be necessary. We will have to love the words and principles of Scripture more than we do our own preferences, family traditions, and cultural norms.

3. Powerful Texts- Exposure of Revolutionary Passages of Scripture

The family reformation in Geneva was text-driven. Calvin brought to light marvelous passages of scripture that inspired a new vision of family life. As he worked through the Bible, he attempted to be faithful to the messages of the text. Rich contours of the theology of family life arose out of the passage itself instead of his philosophy imposing itself upon the text. In this sense, Calvin's family reformation was not philosophy-driven. It was not personality-driven. It was created out of the very words that formed the biblical texts.

It was as if the interacting neutrons and protons of specific words in texts of Scripture activated the atomic fission that exploded across the landscape of family life, ripping into the idols that had disfigured the biblical family in the sixteenth century. In this book alone, we have identified dozens of the texts with which John Calvin dealt with family issues.[4]

4. Doctrinal Precision - a Way of Thinking

The doctrinal precision of the reformation was simply an outgrowth of a particular way of thinking. Simply put, Calvin believed that words, categories, and definitions mattered. This was the mindset that marked the Reformers. This way of thinking, and the doctrinal precision that grows out of it, stands in sharp contrast to the relativistic thinking of today. The reformers took the biblical words, categories and definitions, very seriously. The words were the building blocks of the doctrines that guided the reformation.

It was their way of thinking that embraced a literal interpretation of Scripture on the roles and responsibilities in family life that fomented the family reformation. Steven Lawson illustrates how this worked in Calvin's preaching, "As an expositor, he believed he was not free to play fast and loose with a passage and impose his own meaning on it."[5] This exegetical precision, combined with a passionate desire to conform family life to the contour of Scripture, gave birth to a complete system of biblical categories and practices in the home - because the categories mattered. He argued for the preferred state of marriage, male and female roles in the family and church, male authority and headship in marriage, the obedience of children, the centrality of the home for discipleship, the importance of fathers as teachers, the priority of procreation and large families, and a model of rich investments in one's family for the creation of beautiful home life. Calvin communicated these things on the family extensively through sermons, commentaries, letters, and the registers of the Consistory.

5. A High View of the Family - an Unusual Perspective

Calvin had a high view of the family. Everyone sorts out issues in the order of their importance and it is clear that the Bible communicates a high view of the family. Calvin recognized this and believed the family possessed a sacred status in the world and he argued that it should be treated that way. Therefore, he used very rich and graphic language to explain family life, constantly referring to family relationships as "sacred." He said fathers were "sacred," marriage was "sacred," bonds in the family relationships were "sacred." This very striking language elevates family relationships to a higher level than may be intuitive to our sensibilities or the values of our generation. In reference to marriage, Calvin said, "that sacred bond is especially conspicuous, by which the husband and the wife are combined in one body, and one soul,"[6] and "Among the offices of pertaining to human society, this is the principal one and, as it were, the most sacred, that a man should cleave unto his wife."[7] He spoke of the sacredness of a father-son relationship by stating, "the piety of the son towards his father is to be most assiduously cultivated and ought in itself to be deemed inviolable and sacred."[8] He made it clear that "the name of Father is a sacred one, and is transferred to men by the peculiar goodness of God, the dishonoring of parents redounds to the dishonor of God Himself, nor can anyone despise his father without being guilty of an offense against God."[9] Calvin believed in the sacredness of the authority of parents saying that the "rights of parents are sacred, and not to be violated without the greatest criminality."[10]

Cultures always face two dangers, that of over-exalting the family on the one hand, and making it an idol, or diminishing it so that it loses its biblical priority on the other. While Calvin exalted the family in his time, elevating it higher than his contemporaries, it was not in any way to the exclusion of God or the gospel. The reformation that took place in Geneva threatened to restructure many aspects of the culture, putting down things which had been improperly honored and elevating others to their biblical position in society.

6. Practical Tools - Surge of Written Resources for the Family

With the printing press revolutionizing communication and enabling the mass distribution of material, there were many publications produced which targeted various issues of family life and equipped a new generation in the biblical vision of the Christian home. The theology of the reformers spread like wildfire. Little did the Roman Catholic Johannes Gutenberg realize the way in which his printing press would transform Europe.

In an era when the positions of monk and nun were exalted over fatherhood and motherhood, the Roman Catholic culture was penetrated with tracts, sermons, pamphlets, and books praising marriage and the family. "Housefather" books,[11] catechisms, and etiquette guides were written to correct the old ways. The decisions of the Consistory, as well as expositional sermons in the churches, rang with biblical wisdom that challenged the popish views of family and home. With this outpouring of biblical teaching, the fires of family reformation spread across Europe, bringing down the false doctrines which held the people in bondage to the traditions of men.

7. Tangible Reforms in Real Families - Visible Examples to Follow

Many of the Reformers renovated their own families so that they became pictures of the things which they advocated. Their wives and children experienced the changes that were preached in their sermons and argued for in their letters. They exemplified the theology which they taught and made it clear that sound theology could transform families. Thus, the family reformers stood upon the doctrinal bedrock of the sufficiency of Scripture, not for mere intellectual exercise, but rather for a life-changing journey.

Martin Luther and John Calvin are prime examples of how the practical details of their home lives promoted the reformation about which they preached. We shouldn't minimize the significance of the role that hospitality plays in a reformation. In many ways, the conversations that Luther had around the dinner table effected the reformation as much as, or perhaps even more than, his sermons. That is not to downplay the importance of sermons, but rather to raise the importance of relationships, real-life examples, and practical conversations about biblical ideas. The preaching of the Word is an effective way to transmit didactic teaching, but the changing of lives involves the face-to-face, house-to-house personal application of that teaching.

The marriages of many of the reformers became living epistles of the biblical doctrine of marriage. Historian and pastor James Good reports that Calvin spoke of his wife Idelette as,

"...the excellent companion of his life, the ever faithful assistant of his ministry." He believed what the Bible says, "that whoso findeth a wife, findeth a good thing and obtaineth favor of the Lord."[12]

There she revealed the same beautiful characteristics of a faithful wife. She was devoted to her husband. As he was naturally sickly and weak, she watched by his bedside in sickness, and cheered him in moments of weakness and depression. She thus greatly soothed him in the midst of the tremendous burdens of his labors. Doubtless we owe much of the abundance and clearness of his thoughts to her kind ministry in the home. Often she watched by his bedside at night, holding up his weary head, for he was a terrible sufferer of headache. In his sad hours, when adverse news came, she strengthened and comforted him. When the rebellious raged through the streets crying out against the ministers of Geneva, she retired to her chamber, fell on her knees and prayed. Like a good pastor's wife she visited the sick. She was often seen comforting the sorrowing. Her house was an asylum for the numerous refugees who came crowding to Geneva. She cared for them with such beautiful hospitality that by some she was blamed for being more careful of strangers than of the natives of Geneva. She delighted in the company of his friends, especially of Farel, Beza, and others. She would accompany her husband on his walks, which he took only too rarely, to Cologny and Bellerive. Viret's wife was to her as a sister...[13]

Martin and Katie Luther were also beautiful examples for how family life could be reformed. They had personally departed from the societal ideal to seek the biblical ideal. Church historian Philip Schaff says that,

> They lived happily together for twenty-one years, and shared the usual burdens and joys. Their domestic life is very characteristic, full of good nature, innocent humor, cordial affection, rugged simplicity, and thoroughly German. It falls below the refinement of a modern Christian home, and some of his utterances on the relation between the two sexes are coarse; but we must remember the rudeness of the age, and his peasant origin. No stain rests upon his home life, in which he was as gentle as a lamb and as a child among children.

> "Next to God's Word," he said from his personal experience, "there is no more precious treasure than holy matrimony. God's highest gift on earth is a pious, cheerful, God-fearing, home-keeping wife, with whom you may live peacefully, to whom you may intrust your goods and body and life."

> He loved his wife dearly, and playfully called her in his letters "my heartily beloved, gracious housewife, bound hand and foot in loving service, Catharine, Lady Luther, Lady Doctor, Lady of Zulsdorf, Lady of the Pigmarket, and whatever else she may be." She was a good German Hausfrau, caring for the wants of her husband and children; she contributed to his personal comfort

in sickness and health, and enabled him to exercise his hospitality. She had a strong will, and knew how to take her own part. He sometimes speaks of her as his "Lord Katie," and of himself as her "willing servant." "Katie," he said to her, "you have a pious husband who loves you; you are an empress."[14]

The family reformation was given wings by living examples like John Calvin and Martin Luther. These reformers put into practice those things which they taught. These genuine demonstrations of the practical outworkings of Bible doctrine helped others to see how doctrine applied to everyday life. In their homes, they saw that Christ had spoken deeply into every area of family life and that His words were meant to be put into practice.

These seven igniters were what made the fires of family reformation burn. Let me suggest that these are the basic forces at work in all reformations in all eras.

CHAPTER 4

THE CULTURE CLASHES

The Thunder and Lightning of Family Reformation

I n the same way that thunder blasts and lightning flashes when warm and cold air collide, so there was thunder and lightning when the heat of biblical culture collided with the cold cultures of sixteenth century Europe. The reforms that exploded across the Genevan landscape brought about seismic culture quakes. Calvin's countercultural ideas contradicted well-worn religious practices. Prevailing attitudes toward manhood and womanhood, singleness and marriage, family and church relationships, worldliness and spirituality were challenged. Established patterns were broken. Families were disrupted. As a result of these revolutionary ideas, John Calvin's Geneva was marked by upheaval and transition. What happened in Geneva demonstrated the revolutionary character of the biblical teaching from which the disruptions sprang.

Tumult of Family Reformation

Reformations create tumultuous times because the Word of God divides families, disturbs churches, and judges institutions. Reformations topple our idols and challenge our priorities, belittle our habits, change our schedules, reprioritize our pocketbooks, modify our entertainments, and reform our families. Reformations cause change. They draw a line in the sand. They affect relationships. They result in persecution. This is why the reformation in Scotland, which was fueled by a return to the sufficiency of Scripture, was called "the killing times." Those who desired to live their lives according to the wisdom of God in the area of church life (which was the focus of the Scottish Reformation) were stopped in their tracks by the gibbet and stake. Why? Because the Roman Catholic leaders correctly feared that men who boldly trusted in the sufficiency of Scripture would destabilize their leadership and hegemony over the status quo.

Riots in the Churches

The reformation in Geneva was a time of controversy and sometimes violence - even within church walls. Calvin once had to face libertines armed with swords before the communion table. More than once, after church services, he bared his chest to angry mobs who wanted to kill him. In 1546, riots resulted from attempts to carry the application of the sufficiency of Scripture to the naming of children. Calvin had such a concern for these disruptions that he declared that it might be wise and necessary to post guards at baptisms to keep the peace.[1] The upheaval over the naming of children continued until 1552, when Calvin refused to baptize a child presented by Balthazar Sept. Sept and others were incensed at the policy, saying, "These preachers have insulted us and we will endure it no longer." This particular confrontation ended with three men being held in prison for several days.[2] While we may disagree with some of these applications, we must acknowledge that Calvin sought to transform the church, family, and state by the Word of God. Whenever this is tried, there is a culture clash.

The Offense of Family Reformation

A people who desire to live godly in Christ Jesus will be persecuted because their countercultural lifestyles stick out like a sore thumb. When family patterns are reformed, it is so public that everyone notices. Family, friend, co-worker and church member are easily offended by family reforms. The tumult from the reforms of family life that Calvin experienced in Geneva caused the same kind of turmoil that every father and daughter experience when they change from immodest to modest clothing. I have a friend who received hate mail because he and his daughter objected to modern dating patterns. They determined that she should have her first kiss at the altar instead of in the back seat of a car before marriage. They felt the modern dating patterns of the culture were defiling, so they defied the social structure to be faithful to the biblical commands for sexuality. This attempt at family reform was met with hatred from the Christian community. The truth is, you may get more compassion from church goers if your teen daughter gets pregnant, than if she dresses modestly. Family reformers are an offense to those who fear man and maintain the status quo. When the power of the gospel begins work in our hearts to change us, and then tangible lifestyle changes occur, we become a source of irritation to those who hate the Word of God.

CHAPTER 5

THE DEFINING ISSUES

Where the Battles Raged

*E*very culture has defining issues that need to be addressed by the Word of God and they usually mark the ground upon which spiritual warfare is fought. Spiritual warfare always has its earthly battlegrounds, for where there is no battle, there is no faith. Faith without works is dead. Scripture confronts real issues. It may demand changes in everyday life. It may contradict comfortable practices. It may overthrow parental counsel. It may reject cultural norms. It may challenge well-worn pathways. Battles rage at the crossroads of these issues. In Calvin's Geneva, there were many battlegrounds which exposed the differences between the kingdoms of light and darkness. This understanding is critical for Christian maturity, for the reality is this - reformations are always blood-bought. And, the blood is always spilled around the defining issues of the day.

The battles for family reformation raged on the blood-soaked fields of womanhood, marriage, church and family discipleship, fatherhood, abstinence in marriage, and premarital relationships. The following is a summary of some of the critical defining issues and battles which were fought in the struggle for family reformation in Calvin's Geneva.

Defining Issue #1: Womanhood

Womanhood was a signature battleground during the family reformation. The Reformation era was a tumultuous time in the struggle for the establishment of biblical roles for women. In Geneva, Calvin used Scripture to challenge the attitudes and institutions that incarcerated women behind the bars of ungodly thinking, stripping them of their womanhood. It was a fierce battle for the liberation of women to be wives and mothers. The Roman church forced a philosophy that exalted virginity and seclusion. It devalued home life and deprived women of the husbands and children for which they intuitively longed. As a result of the Reformation, women were liberated from bankrupt systems which distorted their biblically defined roles. The Reformers sought to reestablish women in these roles and put them "securely in homes as wives and mothers…[T]he Reformers believed they had liberated them from sexual repression, cultural deprivation, and male (clerical) domination."[1] Stephen Ozment declares that the Reformation in Europe was the "heyday of the patriarchal nuclear family."[2]

During the Middle Ages and Renaissance period, women were regarded as inferiors to men. As Calvin exposited Scripture, it was plain that husband and wife were intimate partners with different roles and responsibilities. Further, the Catholic system considered marriage to be an inferior and unspiritual state. Canon law argued against marriage and posed the idea that sexual intercourse was always sin, even in marriage. During the late Medieval and early Reformation period, as many as twenty-five percent of the adults were either priests, monks, nuns, or members of celibate trading groups or celibate military service, like the "Teutonic Knights."

One of the key battlegrounds was the convent. Tracts, sermons, and letters waged war against the wicked disfigurements of womanhood, acting as one of the great forces of women's liberation of that day. With the Gutenberg press enabling the wide distribution of printed materials, these publications were often smuggled behind the walls of the convents - to the delight and disturbance of many nuns. When the Reformers compared the cloistered life to Scripture, they found it to be a terrible contradiction of the biblical vision of womanhood, which set women free to become what they were created to be and to experience the pleasures that God had ordained. In his lifetime, Calvin wrote letters to as many as twenty nuns[3] to convince them of the virtues of marriage and the violations that the cloistered life forced upon them. As a result, one of these, Abbess Philippe Chasteigner, fled to Geneva with eight nuns from the monastery of St. Jean de Bonneval.[4]

The Reformers were attacked for doing all they could to get women out of the convents. Martin Luther's ministry to the nuns is showcased in the way he found his wife. Katherine von Bora was secluded from the world as a nun at the Cistercian convent of Nimbschem. "Even relatives who visited were separated by a latticed window from the nuns who were accompanied by an abbess. 'The regulations forbade friendships between the nuns... Silence was the rule...'"[5]

Luther's writings found their way into the nuns' hands, and in 1523, eleven of them managed to escape. The nuns drafted a secret letter to Luther explaining their plight and arranged for fifty-nine-year-old businessman Leonhard Koppe, a local merchant who delivered smoked herring to the convent, to deliver it to him. Upon receiving the letter, Luther made arrangements for the same merchant to make a late-night delivery, and on the back haul bring the nuns out in the empty herring barrels. This was dangerous business, since Duke George had made it a capital crime to "kidnap" nuns. The arrival of the nuns at his home only added to Luther's already mounting challenges. What was he to do with them? One student at Wittenburg chided, "A wagon load of vestal virgins has just come to town all more eager for marriage than for life. May God give them husbands lest worse befall."[6] Luther was able to help all of the women find husbands, except for Katherine von Bora. In an attempt to keep his vow to remain single, he unsuccessfully tried to match her with another man. However, in the end, Katherine von Bora, a woman who had been smuggled out of a convent in a herring barrel, became his wife and was established as a model of godly womanhood and homemaking.

It was a time of liberation from bondage of worldly thinking regarding womanhood. The emphasis on female literacy, companionship and love in marriage, personal salvation, and justification by faith were refreshing winds in a time when the beauty of womanhood was marred.

Defining Issue #2: Marriage

Sparks flew as Calvin challenged many areas of Roman Catholic teaching on marriage. Everything from the nature of marriage to the purpose of marriage to the ceremony of marriage was brought under the lens of Scripture for evaluation. For example, Calvin contradicted the Catholic view of the nature of marriage, fighting tenaciously against the idea that it was a sacrament. He also maintained that marriages could be dissolved under certain circumstances defined in Scripture. Further, Roman Catholic family doctrine valued procreation ahead of affectionate companionship. For Catholics, the purpose of marriage was threefold in order of importance:

1. Procreation

2. Preservation from immorality

3. Companionship

In contrast, the Reformers, and then the Puritans, turned this completely on its head and gave priority to love and companionship:

1. Companionship

2. Preservation from immorality

3. Procreation

This radical change of emphasis not only introduced conflict with established religious values, but it also fostered a greater place for love in the marriage relationship, resulting in a much sweeter home life.

Other reforms were communicated in the Marriage Ordinance of 1546, which dealt with the various issues of marriage such as who can and can't marry, what age they can get married, whether or not divorce is permissible, and more. The marriage ceremony was reformed with a new liturgy. Even the age of marriage was addressed in Geneva. Historically, the average age of marriage is a moving target that rises and falls on the heels of cultural values. It is generally accepted that sixteenth century Europe was experiencing an increase in the age of marriage, with the devaluation of marriage and the monastic system seeming to be among the causes. Calvin, in stark contrast to the monastic traditions all around him, encouraged youthful marriage, believing that marriage was commanded, blessed, and something worth pursuing earlier rather than later.

Robert Kingdon and John Witte, explaining the significance of Calvin's reforms, make it clear that Calvin,

> *"transformed the Western theology and law of sex, marriage, and family life. Building on a generation of Protestant reforms, Calvin constructed a comprehensive new theology and jurisprudence that made marital formation and dissolution, children's nurture and welfare, family cohesion and support, and sexual sin and crime essential concerns for both church and state. Working with other jurists and theologians, Calvin drew the Consistory and Council of Geneva into a creative new alliance to govern domestic and sexual affairs. Together, these authorities outlawed monasticism and mandatory clerical celibacy, and encouraged marriage for all fit adults. They set clear guidelines for courtship and engagement. They mandated parental consent, peer witness, church consecration, and state registration for valid marriage. They radically reconfigured weddings and wedding feasts. They reformed marital property and inheritance, marital consent and impediments. They created new rights and duties for wives within the bedroom and for children within the household. They streamlined the grounds and procedures for annulment. They introduced fault-based divorce for both husbands and wives on grounds of adultery and desertion. They encouraged the remarriage of divorcees and widow(er)s. They punished rape, fornication, prostitution, sodomy, and other sexual*

felonies with startling new severity. They put firm new restrictions on dancing, sumptuousness, ribaldry, and obscenity. They put new stock in catechesis and education, and created new schools, curricula, and teaching aids. They provided new sanctuary to illegitimate, abandoned and abused children. They created new protections for abused wives and impoverished widows."[7]

Defining Issue #3: Church and Family Discipleship

Calvin was disturbed that there were ways in which the Roman Church's relationship with children had ceased to reflect the Biblical pattern. Established practices of church and family discipleship had to be overthrown.

Calvin's baptismal liturgy, designed to correct some of the defaults of the past, helped to define how the community would relate to the spiritual development and discipleship of children. Baptism was to be the beginning of the process of bringing up children in the training and admonition of the Lord. Calvin argues,

> *For we must not lightly overlook the fact, that our Saviour, in ordering little children to be brought to him, adds the reason, "of such is the kingdom of heaven." And he afterwards testifies his good will by act, when he embraces them, and with prayer and benediction commends them to his Father. If it is right that children should be brought*

*to Christ, why should they not be admitted to baptism,
the symbol of our communion and fellowship with Christ?
If the kingdom of heaven is theirs, why should they be
denied the sign by which access, as it were, is opened to
the Church, that being admitted into it they may be
enrolled among the heirs of the heavenly kingdom? How
unjust were we to drive away those whom Christ invites
to himself, to spoil those whom he adorns with his gifts, to
exclude those whom he spontaneously admits. But if we
insist on discussing the difference between our Saviour's
act and baptism, in how much higher esteem shall we hold
baptism, (by which we testify that infants are included
in the divine covenant), than the taking up, embracing,
laying hands on children, and praying over them, acts by
which Christ, when present, declares both that they are
his, and are sanctified by him?*[8]

As Calvin sought to bring baptism under the authority of Scripture,
there were many Roman Catholic practices to overthrow. Karen
Spierling identifies the details of the baptismal practices that were
under scrutiny. According to the old practice,

*[T]he midwife, accompanied by the godparents and a
celebratory party of friends and relatives, would carry
the baby to the church, where the priest would perform
an exorcism at the door and place salt in the child's
mouth. The baptism would proceed with the immersion
of the infant in holy water of the font, and the promise of
baptism would be sealed with chrism. By this rite the child*

was freed from evil spirits, purified of all original sin and sanctified in God's promise of salvation through Christ. In addition, the godmother or godfather might have offered his or her own name as the name of the child, confirming the relationship of spiritual kinship begun on that day.[9]

In contrast, Calvin advocated a different practice, causing upheaval in the sensibilities of the people who had been trained in the Roman Church. Spierling notes,

> *The order of service began with an admonition that the baptism should occur either on Sunday or on another sermon day, 'under the eyes of the whole Congregation.'*
>
> *With this instruction, Calvin established from the start the importance of community participation and witness in the ritual. When the sermon ended, the child was presented. The liturgy did not indicate who was to present the child, and Calvin avoided this issue throughout the description of the ceremony; apparently leaving open the option for either parents or godparents to bring the child forward. He simply indicated that the minister should ask, 'Do you present this child to be baptized?' and the answer should be 'Yes.'*
>
> *After the affirmative response, the minister spoke, defending infant baptism, explaining to the parents and the congregation the important points of the Reformed baptismal doctrine.*[10]

If you isolate the issue of baptism strictly to the controversy of infant baptism versus credo baptism you may miss what Calvin was trying to accomplish. Calvin's infant baptism convictions were undergirded by a number of larger issues. First and foremost was the relationship that would exist between church and family. In Calvin's understanding of Scripture, children were to be completely included in church life for the purpose of discipleship and bringing them up in the fear and admonition of the Lord. At the same time, parents were required to take full responsibility for the spiritual upbringing of the child. The separate jurisdictions of church and family each had their God-ordained, complementary roles in ministry to children. This interplay was defined by the relationships, responsibilities, and covenants made at baptism. For Calvin, infant baptism incorporated the whole family into the life of the church and the whole church into the life of the family.

Defining Issue #4: Fatherhood

Calvin clearly believed that fathers were responsible for the training of children and that current practices needed reform. In view of this, he formulated a catechism in order to facilitate the teaching of doctrine in the homes. The first one, written in 1538, was an in-depth explanation of the truths of the Christian faith. Realizing this was far too complicated for children, he later wrote a children's catechismin question-and-answer format designed to instruct children in basic theology. [11]

The Consistory was used to hold fathers accountable for their responsibilities in child training. Rebukes and even fines were often issued against parents for their children's failure to be able to recite the catechism.

While Calvin correctly understood the responsibility of fathers for the teaching of children and took great pains to establish spiritual life in the homes, it was apparent that all parents did not take that responsibility seriously. In response to this problem, Calvin established the requirement of Sabbath afternoon catechism classes for the children, thus creating a program that displaced the discipleship which was designed for the home. These classes were held at all three of the churches in Geneva at noon, and all the citizens were supposed to attend. Enforcing attendance, though, was often a difficult proposition. In 1549, in order to promote attendance, the Council repeated "its insistence on parental responsibility when it mandated that parents would be fined three solz if they neglected to send their children to catechism."[12]

Calvin's experience in this area reminds us of the concerns of ministers, which gave rise to modern youth ministry, when fathers did not obey the Lord in matters of shepherding their families. The catechism classes were launched as a response to fathers' failure to properly disciple their children, but with their development, other problems soon multiplied.

When fathers refuse to play their roles as the teachers and shepherds of their families, the church often does the same thing Calvin did - it steps in and attempts to pick up the slack through a class or program designed to engage the youth. Even though these practices are well-intentioned, they still overthrow the biblical methods of ministry to children. The problems of youth groups that Calvin faced are the same ones we face today. Gathering youth together without the mentorship of their parents and the relationships of the wider body of the church has always been problematic. It naturally displaces the roles of fathers and exposes the family to other unintended problems.

Defining Issue #5: Abstinence in Marriage

Calvin challenged the status quo regarding sexuality. He was born into a world where sex was considered sinful even between married partners. It was a world where virginity and singleness were glorified and embracing them raised the spiritual and social status of the individual.

Reformation Europe was so confused about the matter that religious authorities suggested 260 days of abstinence per year, "on Thursday in memory of Christ's arrest, on Friday in memory of his death, on Saturday in honour of the Virgin Mary, on Sunday in honour of the Resurrection and on Monday in commemoration of the departed."[13]

In sharp contrast, Calvin's scheme was that sex is good and abstinence in marriage is forbidden except for reasons spelled out in scripture. He affirmed that the Bible tells us that spouses are to have sexual relations regularly and are not to deprive each other, with the only exception being a time of mutual devotion to prayer. "Do not deprive one another, except perhaps by agreement for a limited time, that you may devote yourselves to prayer; but then come together again, so that Satan may not tempt you because of your lack of self-control" (1 Corinthians 7:5).

Defining Issue #6: Premarital Relationships

What role should parents play in the marriages of their children? What kind of authority should children be comfortable with as they are choosing marriage partners? The Consistory addressed every conceivable area of life, including premarital relationships. They determined to use Scripture alone as a guide in all matters, in order to perform a biblical counseling function. They regularly dealt with matters of courtship, engagement, and marriage. Calvin sought to reform every aspect of the premarital relationship using Scripture alone. Kingdon and Witte list the numerous topics which were addressed:

> *Courtship. Individual Consent. Parental Consent. Infancy. Mental Inability. Polygamy. Virginity. Contagion. Sexual Capacity. Age Disparity. Incest. Religious Differences. Marital Property. Premarital Sex. Desertion. Banns. The wedding. These were the main topics of the law and theology of courtship, engagement, and marriage in John Calvin's Geneva. These were the main issues that triggered the scrutiny and activity of the Consistory and the Council. These were the main grounds on which engagements and marriages were made and broken.[14]*

The result of the involvement of the Consistory was the placement of every aspect of the premarital relationship under the glass of Scripture. Calvin uncovered every possible unbiblical practice and sought to reform it, dethroning the dizzying array of practices created by the Roman church and reinstated the simple purity of biblical practices.

SECTION II

CALVIN SPEAKS

CHAPTER 6

The Family as a Foundation

A Means of Grace and Vengeance Across the Generations

C alvin understood that Christian families are the foundation of society. As such they are a conduit of the blessing of God for many generations. He said this fact would be a "consolation to believers, and great ground of terror to the wicked." In regards to the wicked, Calvin defended the just judgment of God in "depriving their families of his grace for many generations" saying, "who will dare to bring a charge against him for this most righteous vengeance?" He acknowledged that the foundation can be so poisoned that the sins of the fathers will be visited upon the following generations. Critical to this understanding was our father Abraham. God brought forth a godly heritage from one generation to the next. As God said to him, "I will make you a great nation; I will bless you and make your name great; And you shall be a blessing. I will bless those who bless you, and I will curse him who curses you; And, in you all the families of the earth shall be blessed" (Genesis 12:2-3). Calvin pointed out that even in His judgments of the ungodly, God "commends the riches of his mercy by extending it to thousands, while he limits his vengeance to four generations." While God works to bless those who love Him, at the same time, He "smites [those who hate Him] with a spirit of madness or folly."

CALVIN SPEAKS:

Mercy To Thousands

On the other hand, there is a promise of mercy to thousands - a promise which is frequently mentioned in Scripture, and forms an article in the solemn covenant made with the Church - I will be "a God unto thee, and to thy seed after thee," (Gen. 17:7). With reference to this, Solomon says, "The just man walketh in his integrity: his children are blessed after him," (Prov. 20:7); not only in consequence of a religious education (though this certainly is by no means unimportant), but in consequence of the blessing promised in the covenant - viz. that the divine favour will dwell forever in the families of the righteous. Herein is excellent consolation to believers, and great ground of terror to the wicked; for if, after death, the mere remembrance of righteousness and iniquity have such an influence on the divine procedure, that his blessing rests on the posterity of the righteous, and his curse on the posterity of the wicked, much more must it rest on the heads of the individuals themselves. Notwithstanding of this, however, the offspring of the wicked sometimes amends, while that of believers degenerates; because the Almighty has not here laid down an inflexible rule which might derogate from his free election. For the consolation of the righteous, and the dismay of the sinner, it is enough that the threatening itself is not vain or nugatory, although it does not always take effect. For, as the temporal punishments inflicted on a few of the wicked are proofs of the divine wrath against sin, and of the future judgment that will ultimately overtake all sinners, though many escape with impunity even to the end of their lives, so, when the Lord gives one example of blessing a son for his father's sake, by visiting him in mercy and kindness, it is a proof of constant and unfailing favour to his worshipers. On the other hand, when, in any single instance, he visits the iniquity of the father on the son, he gives intimation of the judgment which awaits all the reprobate for their own iniquities. The certainty of this is the principal thing here taught. Moreover, the Lord, as it were by the way, commends the riches of his mercy by extending it to thousands, while he limits his vengeance to four generations.[1]

Consolation in Times of Trouble: God's Mercy is Extended from Fathers to Their Children's Children

Wherefore, my beloved brethren, return always to this consolation, that although the wicked strive with all their might to bring ruin upon your Church, and although your faults and offenses have deserved far more than you could ever endure, yet, nevertheless, our Lord will vouchsafe such an outgate to the corrections which he has sent, as that they shall be made helpful to your salvation. His wrath towards his Church, inasmuch as it is only intended to bring her back to well doing, is only for a little moment, and then it passes away, as saith the prophet; his mercy, on the contrary, is eternal, extending to future generations; for from the fathers it descends to their children and to children's children.[2]

Visiting the Iniquity of the Fathers Upon the Children

Thou shalt not bow down thyself unto them, nor serve them: for I the LORD thy God am a jealous God, visiting the iniquity of the fathers upon the children unto the third and fourth generation of them that hate me. - Deuteronomy 5:9

But when God declares that He will cast back the iniquity of the fathers into the bosom of the children, He does not mean that He will take vengeance on poor wretches who have never deserved anything of the sort, but that He is at liberty to punish the crimes of the fathers upon their children and descendants, with the proviso that they too may be justly punished, as being the imitators of their fathers. If any should object, that this is nothing more than to repay every one according to his works, we must remember that, whenever God blinds the children of the ungodly, casts them into a state of reprobation, (conjicit in sesum reprobum), and smites them with a spirit of madness or folly, so that they give themselves up to foul desires, and hasten to their final destruction, - in this way the iniquity of the fathers is visited on their children.[3]

Visiting the Sins of the Fathers upon Following Generations

In the threatening we must attend to what is meant when God declares that he will visit the iniquity of the fathers upon the children unto the third and fourth generation. It seems inconsistent with the equity of the divine procedure to punish the innocent for another's fault; and the Lord himself declares, that "the son shall not bear the iniquity of the father," (Ezek. 18:20). But still we meet more than once with a declaration as to the postponing of the punishment of the sins of fathers to future generations. Thus Moses repeatedly addresses the Lord as "visiting the iniquity of the fathers upon the children unto the third and fourth generation," (Num. 14:18). In like manner, Jeremiah, "Thou showest loving-kindness unto thousands, and recompenses the iniquity of the fathers into the bosom of their children after them" (Jer. 32:18). Some feeling sadly perplexed how to solve this difficulty, think it is to be understood of temporal punishments only, which it is said sons may properly bear for the sins of their parents, because they are often inflicted for their own safety. This is indeed true; for Isaiah declared to Hezekiah, that his children should be stript of the kingdom, and carried away into captivity, for a sin which he had committed (Isa. 39:7); and the households of Pharaoh and Abimelech were made to suffer for an injury done to Abraham (Gen. 12:17;

20:3–18). But the attempt to solve the question in this way is an evasion rather than a true interpretation. For the punishment denounced here and in similar passages is too great to be confined within the limits of the present life. We must therefore understand it to mean, that a curse from the Lord righteously falls not only on the head of the guilty individual, but also on all his lineage. When it has fallen, what can be anticipated but that the father, being deprived of the Spirit of God, will live most flagitiously; that the son, being in like manner forsaken of the Lord, because of his father's iniquity, will follow the same road to destruction; and be followed in his turn by succeeding generations, forming a seed of evil-doers?

First, let us examine whether such punishment is inconsistent with the divine justice. If human nature is universally condemned, those on whom the Lord does not bestow the communication of his grace must be doomed to destruction; nevertheless, they perish by their own iniquity, not by unjust hatred on the part of God. There is no room to expostulate, and ask why the grace of God does not forward their salvation as it does that of others. Therefore, when God punishes the wicked and flagitious for their crimes, by depriving their families of his grace for many generations, who will dare to bring a charge against him for this most righteous vengeance? But it will be said, the Lord, on the contrary, declares, that the son shall not suffer for the father's sin (Ezek. 18:20). Observe the scope of that passage. The Israelites, after being subjected to a long period of uninterrupted calamities, had begun to say, as a proverb, that their fathers had eaten the sour grape, and thus set the children's teeth on edge; meaning that they, though in themselves righteous and innocent, were paying the penalty of sins committed by their parents, and this more from the implacable anger than the duly tempered severity of God. The prophet declares it was not so: that they were punished for their own wickedness; that it was not in accordance with the justice of God that a righteous son should suffer for the iniquity of a wicked father; and that nothing of the kind was exemplified in what they suffered. For, if the visitation of which we now speak is accomplished when God withdraws from the children of the wicked the light of his truth and the other helps to salvation, the only way in which they are accursed for their fathers' wickedness is in being blinded and abandoned by God, and so left to walk in their parents' steps. The misery which they suffer in time, and the destruction to which they are finally doomed, are thus punishments inflicted by divine justice, not for the sins of others, but for their own iniquity.[4]

CHAPTER 7

THE SWEETNESS
OF MARRIAGE

A Sacred Bond with
Two Under One Name

Whether he was soaring with wonder at its glories or lashing out in belittling anger against those who would contradict the heart of God on the matter, Calvin tenaciously upheld the high view and sweet nature of biblical marriage. He intentionally sought to reform marriage against the prevailing sour tide of a Roman Catholic canon law. For him, Scripture was sufficient for understanding marriage and he denounced "the Church's commendation of celibacy, toleration of secret marriages, celebration of marriage as a sacrament, swollen roll of impediments to marriage, prohibition of divorce, and counsel against remarriage."[1] Calvin derived principles from Scripture for everything concerning marriage including the age of marriage, the premarital relationship, the courtship, the proposal of marriage, and the marriage ceremony itself. While the Roman Church taught that marriage was the least fruitful estate, Calvin believed it was the most fruitful. He pointed out that the command, "be fruitful and multiply" (Genesis 1:28) was the first command in Scripture before the fall and therefore was in force after Adam and Eve were driven from the garden.

Calvin emphasized the seriousness of marriage and the necessity of protecting its integrity since God Himself was its Author. In order to ensure the legitimacy of a marriage and to provide a good foundation for it, he required that marriage be authorized with the involvement and affirmation of the parents, the family, the civil magistrate, the friends (witnesses), and the church.

CALVIN SPEAKS:

God - The Author and Patron of Marriage

And the rib, which the Lord God had taken from man, made he a woman, and brought her unto the man. - Genesis 2:22

Moses now relates that marriage was divinely instituted, which is especially useful to be known; for since Adam did not take a wife to himself at his own will, but received her as offered and appropriated to him by God, the sanctity of marriage hence more clearly appears, because we recognize God as its Author. The more Satan has endeavored to dishonor marriage, the more should we vindicate it from all reproach and abuse, that it may receive its due reverence...[B]y showing the dignity of marriage, we must remove superstition, lest it should in the slightest degree hinder the faithful from chastely using the lawful and pure ordinance of God; and further, we must oppose the lasciviousness of the flesh, in order that men may live modestly with their wives. But if no other reason influenced us, yet this alone ought to be abundantly sufficient, that unless we think and speak honorably of marriage, reproach is attached to its Author and Patron, for such God is here described as being by Moses.[2]

Not Profitable to Be Alone

It is not good that the man should be alone... - Genesis 2:18

Moses now explains the design of God in creating the woman; namely, that there should be human beings on the earth who might cultivate mutual society between themselves. Yet a doubt may arise whether this design ought to be extended to progeny, for the words simply mean that since it was not expedient for man to be alone, a wife must be created, who might be his helper. I, however, take the meaning to be this, that God begins, indeed, at the first step of human society, yet designs to include others, each in its proper place. The commencement, therefore, involves a general principle, that man was formed to be a social animal. Now, the human race could not exist without the woman; and, therefore, in the conjunction of human beings, that sacred bond is especially conspicuous, by which the husband and the wife are combined in one body, and one soul; as nature itself taught Plato, and others of the sounder class of philosophers, to speak. But although God pronounced, concerning Adam, that it would not be profitable for him to be alone, yet I do not restrict the declaration to his person alone, but rather regard it as a common law of man's vocation, so that everyone ought to receive it as said to himself, that solitude is not good, excepting only him whom God exempts as by a special privilege. Many think that celibacy conduces to their advantage, and therefore, abstain from marriage, lest they should be miserable. Not only have heathen writers defined that to be a happy life which is passed without a wife, but the first book of Jerome, against Jovinian, is stuffed with petulant reproaches, by which he attempts to render hallowed wedlock both hateful and infamous. To these wicked suggestions of Satan let the faithful learn to oppose [with the] declaration of God, by which he ordains the conjugal life for man, not to his destruction, but to his salvation.[3]

What Does It Mean to Leave and Cleave?

Therefore shall a man leave his father and his mother, and shall cleave unto his wife: and they shall be one flesh. - Genesis 2:24

The sum of the whole is, that among the offices pertaining to human society, this is the principal, and as it were the most sacred, that a man should cleave unto his wife. And he amplifies this by a superadded comparison, that the husband ought to prefer his wife to his father. But the father is said to be left not because marriage severs sons from their fathers, or dispenses with other ties of nature, for in this way God would be acting contrary to himself. While, however, the piety of the son towards his father is to be most assiduously cultivated and ought in itself to be deemed inviolable and sacred, yet Moses so speaks of marriage as to show that it is less lawful to desert a wife

*than parents. Therefore, they who, for slight causes, rashly
allow of divorces, violate, in one single particular, all the
laws of nature, and reduce them to nothing. If we should
make it a point of conscience not to separate a father from
his son, it is a still greater wickedness to dissolve the bond
which God has preferred to all others.[4]*

The Two Shall Become One

*Therefore shall a man leave his father and his mother, and shall cleave unto his wife:
and they shall be one flesh. - Genesis 2:24*

*Although the ancient Latin interpreter has translated
the passage 'in one flesh,' yet the Greek interpreters have
expressed it more forcibly: 'They two shall be into one
flesh,' and thus Christ cites the place in Matthew 19:5.
But though here no mention is made of two, yet there is
no ambiguity in the sense; for Moses had not said that
God has assigned many wives, but only one to one man;
and in the general direction given, he had put the wife
in the singular number. It remains, therefore, that the
conjugal bond subsists between two persons only, whence
it easily appears, that nothing is less accordant with the
divine institution than polygamy. Now, when Christ, in
censuring the voluntary divorces of the Jews, adduces as
his reason for doing it, that 'it was not so in the beginning,'
(Matthew 19:5) he certainly commands this institution
to be observed as a perpetual rule of conduct. To the same*

point also Malachi recalls the Jews of his own time: "Did he not make them one from the beginning? And yet the Spirit was abounding in him" (Malachi 2:15).[5]

Two Under One Name

Male and female created he them; and blessed them, and called their name Adam, in the day when they were created. - Genesis 5:2

This clause commends the sacred bond of marriage, and the inseparable union of the husband and the wife. For when Moses has mentioned only one, he immediately afterwards includes both under one name. And he assigns a common name indiscriminately to both, in order that posterity might learn more sacredly to cherish this connection between each other, when they saw that their first parents were denominated as one person. The trifling inference of Jewish writers, that married persons only are called Adam (or man), is refuted by the history of the creation; nor truly did the Spirit, in this place, mean anything else, than that after the appointment of marriage, the husband and the wife were like one man. Moreover, he records the blessing pronounced upon them, that we may observe in it the wonderful kindness of God in continuing to grant it; yet let us know that by the depravity and wickedness of men it was, in some degree, interrupted.[6]

Marriage a Covenant - United by God's Authority

Yet ye say, Wherefore? Because the LORD hath been witness between thee and the wife of thy youth, against whom thou hast dealt treacherously: yet is she thy companion, and the wife of thy covenant. - Malachi 2:14

But in order to press the matter more on the priests, he calls their attention to the fact that God is the founder of marriage. Testified has Jehovah, he says, between thee and thy wife…He intimates in these words, that when a marriage takes place between a man and a woman, God presides and requires a mutual pledge from both. Hence Solomon, in Proverbs 2:17, calls marriage the covenant of God, for it is superior to all human contracts. So also Malachi declares, that God is as it were the stipulator, who by his authority joins the man to the woman, and sanctions the alliance: God then has testified between thee and thy wife, as though he had said, "Thou hast violated not only all human laws, but also the compact which God himself has consecrated, and which ought justly to be deemed more sacred than all other compacts: as then God has testified between thee and thy wife, and thou now deceivest her, how darest thou to come to the altar? And how canst thou think that God will be pleased with thy sacrifices or regard thy oblations?"[7]

The Divine Good in the Order of Marriage

It is not good that the man should be alone;
I will make him an help meet for him. - Genesis 2:18

Therefore, amidst many inconveniences of marriage, which are the fruits of degenerate nature, some residue of divine good remains; as in the fire apparently smothered, some sparks still glitter. On this main point hangs another, that women, being instructed in their duty of helping their husbands, should study to keep this divinely appointed order. It is also the part of men to consider what they owe in return to the other half of their kind, for the obligation of both sexes is mutual, and on this condition is the woman assigned as a help to the man, that he may fill the place of her head and leader.[8]

Obligations of Marriage

So ought men to love their wives as their own bodies: he that loveth his wife loveth himself. For no man ever yet hated his own flesh; but nourisheth and cherisheth it, even as the Lord the church. - Ephesians 5:28-29

Even as Christ the church. He proceeds to enforce the obligations of marriage by representing to us Christ and his Church; for a more powerful example could not have been adduced. The strong affection which a husband ought to cherish towards his wife is exemplified by Christ, and an instance of that unity which belongs to marriage is declared to exist between himself and the Church. This is a remarkable passage on the mysterious intercourse which we have with Christ.[9]

The Dignity of Marriage

Paul enumerates marriage among the qualities of a bishop; those men declare that, in the ecclesiastical order, marriage is an intolerable vice; and, indeed, not content with this general vituperation, they term it, in their canons, the uncleanness and pollution of the flesh (Siric. ad Episc. Hispaniar.). Let everyone consider with himself from what forge these things have come. Christ deigns so to honour marriage as to make it an image of his sacred union with the Church. What greater eulogy could be pronounced on the dignity of marriage? How, then, dare they have the effrontery to give the name of unclean and polluted to that which furnishes a bright representation of the spiritual grace of Christ?[10]

Christ's High View of Marriage

And the third day there was a marriage in Cana of Galilee; and the mother of Jesus was there: And both Jesus was called, and his disciples, to the marriage. - John 2:1-2

It was probably one of Christ's near relations who married a wife; for Jesus is mentioned as having accompanied his mother...It is a high honor given to marriage, that Christ not only deigned to be present at a nuptial banquet, but honored it with his first miracle. There are some ancient Canons which forbid the clergy to attend a marriage. The reason of the prohibition was, that by being the spectators of the wickedness which was usually practiced on such occasions, they might in some measure be regarded as approving of it. But it would have been far better to carry to such places so much gravity as to restrain the licentiousness in which unprincipled and abandoned men indulge, when they are withdrawn from the eyes of others. Let us, on the contrary, take Christ's example for our rule; and let us not suppose that anything else than what we read that he did can be profitable to us.[11]

The Example of the Apostles in Mixing Ministry and Marriage

Wherefore the apostle declares distinctly, without reservation, "Marriage is honourable in all, and the bed undefiled; but whoremongers and adulterers God will judge" (Heb. 13:4). And the apostles showed, by their own example, that marriage is not unbefitting the holiness of any function, however excellent; for Paul declares, that they not only retained their wives, but led them about with them (1 Cor. 9:5).[12]

Prohibition of Marriage - an Idea for Heretics

Paul terms the prohibition of marriage a doctrine of devils (1 Tim. 4:1, 3); and the Spirit elsewhere declares that "marriage is honourable in all" (Heb. 13:4). Having afterwards interdicted their priests from marriage, they insist on this as a true and genuine interpretation of Scripture, though nothing can be imagined more alien to it. Should any one venture to open his lips in opposition, he will be judged a heretic, since the determination of the Church is without challenge, and it is unlawful to have any doubt as to the accuracy of her interpretation.[13]

Calvin's Attack of Catholic Law on Marriage

The last of all is marriage, which, while all admit it to be an institution of God, no man ever saw to be a sacrament, until the time of Gregory. And would it ever have occurred to the mind of any sober man? It is a good and holy ordinance of God. And agriculture, architecture, shoemaking, and shaving, are lawful ordinances of God; but they are not sacraments. For in a sacrament, the thing required is not only that it be a work of God, but that it be an external ceremony appointed by God to confirm a promise. That there is nothing of the kind in marriage, even children can judge. But it is a sign, they say, of a sacred thing, that is, of the spiritual union of Christ with the Church. If by the term sign they understand a symbol set before us by God to assure us of our faith, they wander widely from the mark. If they mean merely a sign because it has been employed as a similitude, I will show how acutely they reason. Paul says, "One star differeth from another star in glory. So also is the resurrection of the dead" (1 Corinthians 15:41, 42). Here is one sacrament. Christ says, "The kingdom of heaven is like to a grain of mustard seed" (Matthew 13:31). Here is another sacrament. Again, "The kingdom of heaven is like unto heaven" (Matthew 13:33). Here is a third sacrament. Isaiah says, "He shall feed his flock like a shepherd" (Isaiah 40:11). Here is a fourth sacrament. In another passage he says, "The Lord shall go forth as a mighty man" (Isaiah 13:13). Here is a fifth sacrament. And where will be the end or limit? Everything in this way will be a sacrament. All the parables and similitudes in Scripture will be so many sacraments. Nay, even theft will be a sacrament, seeing it is written, "The day of the Lord so cometh as a thief in the night" (1 Thessalonians 5:2). Who can tolerate the ignorant garrulity of these sophists? I admit, indeed, that whenever we see a vine, the best thing is to call to mind what our Savior says, "I am the true vine, and my father is the husbandman." "I am the vine, ye are the branches" (John 15:1, 5). And whenever we meet a shepherd with his flock, it is good also to remember, "I am the good shepherd, and know my sheep, and am known of mine" (John 10:14). But any man who would class such similitudes with sacraments should be sent to bedlam.

They adduce the words of Paul, by which they say that the name of a sacrament is given to marriage, "He that loveth his wife loveth himself. For no man ever yet hated his own flesh; but nourisheth and cherisheth it, even as the Lord the Church: for we are members of his body, of his flesh, and of his bones. For this cause shall a man leave a father and mother, and shall be joined unto his wife, and they two shall be one flesh. This is a great mystery: but I speak concerning Christ and the Church" (Ephesians 5:28, 32). To treat Scripture thus is to confound heaven and earth. Paul, in order to show husbands how they ought to love their wives, sets Christ before them as an example. As he shed his bowels of affection for the Church, which he has espoused to himself, so he would have everyone to feel affected toward his wife. Then he adds, "He that loveth his wife loveth himself," "even as the Lord the Church." Moreover, to show how Christ loved the Church as himself, nay, how he made himself one with his spouse the Church, he applies to her what Moses relates that Adam said of himself. For after Eve was brought into his presence, knowing that she had been formed out of his side, he exclaimed, "This is now bone of my bones, and flesh of my flesh" (Genesis 2:23). That all this was spiritually fulfilled in Christ, and in us, Paul declares, when he says, that we are members of his body, of his flesh, and of his bones, and so one flesh with him. At length he breaks out into the exclamation, "This is a great mystery;" and lest anyone should be misled by the ambiguity, he says, that he is not speaking of the connection between husband and wife, but of the spiritual marriage of Christ and the Church. And truly it is a great mystery that Christ allowed a rib to be taken from himself, of which we might be formed; that is, that when he was strong, he was pleased to become weak, that we might be strengthened by his strength, and should no longer live ourselves, but he live in us (Galatians 2:20).

The thing which misled them was the term sacrament. But, was it right that the whole Church should be punished for the ignorance of these men? Paul called it a mystery. When the Latin interpreter might have abandoned this mode of expression as uncommon to Latin ears, or converted it into "secret," he preferred calling it Sacramentum, but in no other sense than the Greek term musthrion was used by Paul. Let them go now and clamor against skill in languages, their ignorance of which leads them most shamefully astray in a matter easy and obvious to everyone. But why do they so strongly urge the term sacrament in this one passage, and in others pass it by with neglect? For both in the First Epistle to Timothy (1 Timothy 3:9, 16), and also in the Epistle to the Ephesians, it is used by the Vulgate interpreter, and in every instance, for mystery. Let us, however, pardon them this lapsus, though liars ought to have good memories. Marriage being thus recommended by the title of a sacrament, can it be anything but vertiginous levity afterwards to call it uncleanness, and pollution, and carnal defilement? How absurd is it to debar priests from a sacrament if they say that they debar not from a sacrament but from carnal connection, they will not thus escape me. They say that this connection is part of the sacrament, and thereby figures the union which we have with Christ in conformity of nature, inasmuch as it is by this connection that husband and wife become one flesh; although some have here found two sacraments, the one of God and the soul, in bridegroom and bride, another of Christ and the Church, in husband and wife. Be this as it may, this connection is a sacrament from which no Christian can lawfully be debarred, unless, indeed, the sacraments of Christians accord so ill that they cannot stand together. There is also another absurdity in these dogmas. They affirm that in a sacrament the gift of the Holy Spirit is conferred; this connection they hold to be a sacrament, and yet they deny that in it the Holy Spirit is ever present.

And, that they might not delude the Church in this matter merely, what a long series of errors, lies, frauds, and iniquities have they appended to one error? So that you may say they sought nothing but a hiding-place for abominations when they converted marriage into a sacrament. When once they obtained this, they appropriated to themselves the cognizance of conjugal causes: as the thing was spiritual, it was not to be intermeddled with by profane judges. Then they enacted laws by which they confirmed their tyranny, - laws partly impious toward God, partly fraught with injustice toward men; such as, that marriages contracted between minors, without the consent of their parents, should be valid; that no lawful marriages can be contracted between relations within the seventh degree, and that such marriages, if contracted, should be dissolved. Moreover, they frame degrees of kindred contrary to the laws of all nations, and even the polity of Moses, and enact that a husband who has repudiated an adulteress may not marry again - that spiritual kindred cannot be joined in marriage - that marriage cannot be celebrated from Septuagesimo to the Octaves of Easter, three weeks before the nativity of John, nor from Advent to Epiphany, and innumerable others, which it were too tedious to mention. We must now get out of their mire, in which our discourse has stuck longer than our inclination. Methinks, however, that much has been gained if I have, in some measure, deprived these asses of their lion's skin.[14]

Against the Oath of Celibacy

Thus it is that God, by fearful examples, punishes the audacity of men, when, unmindful of their infirmity, they, against nature, affect that which has been denied to them, and despising the remedies which the Lord has placed in their hands, are confident in their ability to overcome the disease of incontinence by contumacious obstinacy. For what other name can we give it, when a man, admonished of his need of marriage, and of the remedy with which the Lord has thereby furnished, not only despises it, but binds himself by an oath to despise it?[15]

Doctrines of Devils for Marriage

I omit Paul's injunction, in numerous passages, that a bishop be the husband of one wife; but what could be stronger than his declaration, that in the latter days there would be impious men "forbidding to marry" (1 Tim. 4:3)? Such persons he calls not only impostors, but devils. We have therefore a prophecy, a sacred oracle of the Holy Spirit, intended to warn the Church from the outset against perils, and declaring that the prohibition of marriage is a doctrine of devils. They think that they get finely off when they wrest this passage, and apply it to Montanus, the Tatians, the Encratites, and other ancient heretics. These (they say) alone condemned marriage; we by no means condemn it, but only deny it to the ecclesiastical order, in whom we think it not befitting.[16]

CHAPTER 8

THE HUSBAND'S STRONG AFFECTION

No Ordinary Love

C alvin believed in patriarchal headship of a husband over
his wife and taught that headship must be sweet and
nurturing, saturated with tenderness and love, full of service, and
exemplifying the caring headship of Christ over His own bride the
Church. In our day, the term patriarchy is used as a perjorative by
many people. But for Calvin, the behaviors associated with male
leadership, headship, and husbandry were the behaviors of Christ
toward His bride. He taught that male headship should be a
comfort to wives and that husbands should, "cherish toward their
wives no ordinary love." He branded men as "monsters" if they
did not have toward their wives the affection and gentleness of

Christ. He recognized that men were enjoined by God "to love and to spare" their wives "as the weaker vessels." What kind of love? What kind of patriarchy? It was nothing but the love and headship of Christ!

Calvin Speaks:

What Kind of Love Must a Husband Give?

Husbands, love your wives, even as Christ also loved the church, and gave himself for it. - Ephesians 5:25

From husbands, on the other hand, the apostle requires that they cherish toward their wives no ordinary love; for to them, also, he holds out the example of Christ, - even as Christ also loved the church. If they are honored to bear his image, and to be, in some measure, his representatives, they ought to resemble him also in the discharge of duty.

And gave himself for it. This is intended to express the strong affection which husbands ought to have for their wives, though he takes occasion, immediately afterwards, to commend the grace of Christ. Let husbands imitate Christ in this respect, that he scrupled not to die for his church. One peculiar consequence, indeed, which resulted from his death, - that by it he redeemed his church, - is altogether beyond the power of men to imitate.[1]

One Flesh - Loving and Hating Your Own Body

They adduce the words of Paul, by which they say that the name of a sacrament is given to marriage, "He that loveth his wife loveth himself. For no man ever yet hated his own flesh; but nourisheth and cherisheth it, even as the Lord the Church: for we are members of his body, of his flesh, and of his bones. For this cause shall a man leave his father and mother, and shall be joined unto his wife, and they two shall be one flesh. This is a great mystery: but I speak concerning Christ and the Church" (Eph. 5:28, 32). To treat Scripture thus is to confound heaven and earth. Paul, in order to show husbands how they ought to love their wives, sets Christ before them as an example. As he shed his bowels of affection for the Church, which he has espoused to himself, so he would have everyone to feel affected toward his wife. Then he adds, "He that loveth his wife loveth himself," "even as the Lord the Church." Moreover, to show how Christ loved the Church as himself, nay, how he made himself one with his spouse the Church, he applies to her what Moses relates that Adam said of himself. For after Eve was brought into his presence, knowing that she had been formed out of his side, he exclaimed, "This is now bone of my bones, and flesh of my flesh" (Gen. 2:23). That all this was spiritually fulfilled in Christ, and in us, Paul declares, when he says, that we are members of his body, of his flesh, and of his bones, and so one flesh with him. At length he breaks out into the exclamation, "This is a great mystery;" and lest anyone should be misled by the ambiguity, he says, that he is not speaking of the connection between husband and wife, but of the spiritual marriage of Christ and the Church. And truly it is a great mystery that Christ allowed a rib to be taken from himself, of which we might be formed; that is, that when he was strong, he was pleased to become weak, that we might be strengthened by his strength, and should no longer live ourselves, but he live in us (Gal. 2:20).[2]

Who Is "The Savior of the Body"?

For the husband is the head of the wife, even as Christ is the head of the church: and he is the Saviour of the body. - Ephesians 5:23

The pronoun He (αὐτός) is supposed by some to refer to Christ; and, by others, to the husband. It applies more naturally, in my opinion, to Christ, but still with a view to the present subject. In this point, as well as in others, the resemblance ought to hold. As Christ rules over his church for her salvation, so nothing yields more advantage or comfort to the wife than to be subject to her husband. To refuse that subjection, by means of which they might be saved, is to choose destruction.[3]

Male Headship Explained

For the man is not of the woman; but the woman of the man. - I Corinthians 11:8

He establishes by two arguments for the pre-eminence, which he had assigned to men above women. The first is, that as the woman derives her origin from the man, she is therefore inferior in rank. The second is, that as the woman was created for the sake of the man, she is therefore subject to him, as the work ultimately produced is to its cause. That the man is the beginning of the woman and the end for which she was made, is evident from the law (Genesis 2:18).[4]

A Husband's Headship Resembles Christ's

This is the reason assigned why wives should be obedient. Christ has appointed the same relation to exist between a husband and a wife, as between himself and his church. This comparison ought to produce a stronger impression on their minds, than the mere declaration that such is the appointment of God. Two things are here stated. God has given to the husband authority over the wife; and a resemblance of this authority is found in Christ, who is the head of the church, as the husband is of the wife.[5]

A Husband's Protection of His Wife

For that as much as was in him, he laid his wife open to be defiled. And why so? We have seen before that the husband ought to be as a veil or coverture to his wife. When a woman shall be married, and that her husband shall live with her doing his duty, this is to the end, she may be there as it were in safeguard, and that none come to deceive nor defile her. Now therefore Isaac, for the discharging of his duty, ought to have been as a veil or coverture to his wife: that is to say, under the name of a husband and of marriage: he ought to have let that none should have attempted to withdraw her, whether it were to have her to wife, or after any other manner: For marriage is as a safeguard, (as we have said) and God would have it honored in all ages.[6]

The Man is a Monster
Who Does Not Love His Wife

So ought men to love their wives as their own bodies.
He that loveth his wife loveth himself. - Ephesians 5:28

He that loveth his wife. An argument is now drawn from nature itself, to prove that men ought to love their wives. Every man, by his very nature, loves himself. But no man can love himself without loving his wife. Therefore, the man who does not love his wife is a monster. The minor *proposition is proved in this manner. Marriage was appointed by God on the condition that the two should be one flesh; and that this unity may be the more sacred, he again recommends it to our notice by the consideration of Christ and his church. Such is the amount of his argument, which to a certain extent applies universally to human society. To shew what man owes to man, Isaiah says, "hide not thyself from thine own flesh." (Isaiah 58:7) But this refers to our common nature. Between a man and his wife there is a far closer relation; for they not only are united by a resemblance of nature, but by the bond of marriage have become one man. Whoever considers seriously the design of marriage cannot but love his wife.*[7]

The Danger of Tyranny in Marriage

Wives, submit yourselves unto your own husbands, as it is fit in the Lord. Husbands, love your wives, and be not bitter against them. - Colossians 3:18-19

He commands wives to be subject. He requires love on the part of husbands, and that they be not bitter, because there is a danger lest they should abuse their authority in the way of tyranny.[8]

Degrees of Union - Marriage More Sacred Than Other Relationships

For this cause shall a man leave his father and mother, and shall be joined unto his wife, and they two shall be one flesh. - Ephesians 5:31

He shall leave his father and mother. As if he had said, "Let him rather leave his father and mother than not cleave to his wife." The marriage bond does not set aside the other duties of mankind, nor are the commandments of God so inconsistent with each other, that a man cannot be a good and faithful husband without ceasing to be a dutiful son. It is altogether a question of degree. Moses draws the comparison, in order to express more strongly the close and sacred union which subsists between husband and wife. A son is bound by an inviolable law of nature to perform his duties towards his father; and when the obligations of a husband towards his wife are declared to be stronger, their force is the better understood. He who resolves to be a good husband will not fail to perform his filial duties, but will regard marriage as more sacred than all other ties. And they two shall be one flesh. They shall be one man, or, to use a common phrase, they shall constitute one person; which certainly would not hold true with regard to any other kind of relationship. All depends on this, that the wife was formed of the flesh and bones of her husband. Such is the union between us and Christ, who in some sort makes us partakers of his substance. "We are bone of his bone, and flesh of his flesh," (Genesis 2:23) not because, like ourselves, he has a human nature, but because, by the power of his Spirit, he makes us a part of his body, so that from him we derive our life.[9]

A WIFE
THE DISTINGUISHED
ORNAMENT OF MAN

That the Sweetest Harmony Would Reign

*F*eminists tell us that a wife under submission is a doormat and a slave. Calvin believed otherwise. He viewed a wife's submission as a wonderful grace and her finest contribution to her husband. For Calvin, a wife was a tool in the hand of the Lord to be a comfort and help to her husband as the "inseparable associate of his life." She was not created to be a doormat, but rather "a faithful assistant to him." Her calling in life was to "cultivate a holy, as well as friendly and peaceful" life for her husband. Calvin reminds us that "Sarah was a great solace to our father Abraham" and that God had created man and woman to "cultivate a holy, as well as friendly and peaceful intercourse."

Calvin extolled the beauty of womanhood declaring that "the woman is a distinguished ornament of the man" and that "it is a great honor that God has appointed her to the man as the partner of his life." God had created marriage in such a way that "the sweetest harmony would reign" in it, and though the fall had brought trials and hardships, "marriage was not capable of being so far vitiated by the depravity of men, that the blessing which God has once sanctioned by his word should be utterly abolished and extinguished." Calvin's own marriage was an example of this. When his wife died, he said, "I have been bereaved of the best companion of my life."

CALVIN SPEAKS:

The Woman Is a Distinguished Ornament of the Man

For a man indeed ought not to cover his head, forasmuch as he is the image and glory of God: but the woman is the glory of the man. For the man is not of the woman; but the woman of the man. - I Corinthians 11:7-8

The woman is the glory of the man. There is no doubt that the woman is a distinguished ornament of the man; for it is a great honor that God has appointed her to the man as the partner of his life, and a helper to him, and has made her subject to him as the body is to the head. For what Solomon affirms as to a careful wife - that she is a crown to her husband, (Proverbs 12:4) is true of the whole sex, if we look to the appointment of God, which Paul here commends, showing that the woman was created for this purpose - that she might be a distinguished ornament of the man.[1]

Eve - The Inseparable Associate of Adam's Life

I will make him an help meet for him. - Genesis 2:18

In the Hebrew it is (kenegedo,) "as if opposite to," or "over against him." (Caph) in that language is a note of similitude. But although some of the Rabbis think it is here put as an affirmative, yet I take it in its general sense, as though it were said that she is a kind of counterpart, (ἀντίστοικον, or ἀντίστροφον;) for the woman is said to be opposite to or over against the man, because she responds to him. But the particle of similitude seems to me to be added because it is a form of speech taken from common usage. The Greek translators have faithfully rendered the sense, Κατ'' αὐτόν; and Jerome, "Which may be like him," for Moses intended to note some equality. And hence is refitted the error of some, who think that the woman was formed only for the sake of propagation, and who restrict the word "good," which had been lately mentioned, to the production of offspring. They do not think that a wife was personally necessary for Adam, because he was hitherto free from lust; as if she had been given to him only for the companion of his chamber, and not rather that she might be the inseparable associate of his life. Wherefore the particle (caph) is of importance, as intimating that marriage extends to all parts and usages of life. The explanation given by others, as if it were said, "Let her be ready to obedience," is cold; for Moses intended to express more, as is manifest from what follows.[2]

A Wife - The Man's Consort and Companion

Yet ye say, Wherefore? Because the LORD hath been witness between thee and the wife of thy youth, against whom thou hast dealt treacherously: yet is she thy companion, and the wife of thy covenant. - Malachi 2:14

He calls her a consort, or companion, or associate, because marriage, we know, is contracted on this condition - that the wife is to become as it were the half part of the man... The wife of thy covenant is to be taken for a covenanted wife, that is, "The wife who has been united to thee by God's authority, that there might be no separation; but all integrity is violated, and as if it were abolished."[3]

"The Best Companion of My Life"
Written Upon the Death of Calvin's Wife

And truly mine is no common source of grief. I have been bereaved of the best companion of my life, of one who, had it been so ordered, would not only have been the willing sharer of my indigence, but even of my death. During her life she was the faithful helper of my ministry. From her I never experienced the slightest hindrance. She was never troublesome to me throughout the entire course of her illness; she was more anxious about her children than about herself. As I feared these private cares might annoy her to no purpose, I took occasion, on the third day before her death, to mention that I would not fail in discharging my duty to her children. Taking up the matter immediately, she said, "I have already committed them to God." When I said that that was not to prevent me from caring for them, she replied, "I know you will not neglect what you know has been committed to God."[4]

A Companion and Associate for the Sweetest Harmony in Marriage

Now, since God assigns the woman as a help to the man, he not only prescribes to wives the rule of their vocation to instruct them in their duty, but he also pronounces that marriage will really prove to men the best support of life. We may therefore conclude that the order of nature implies that the woman should be the helper of the man. The vulgar proverb, indeed, is, that she is a necessary evil; but the voice of God is rather to be heard, which declares that woman is given as a companion and an associate to the man, to assist him to live well. I confess, indeed, that in this corrupt state of mankind, the blessing of God, which is here described, is neither perceived nor flourishes; but the cause of the evil must be considered, namely, that the order of nature, which God had appointed, has been inverted by us. For if the integrity of man had remained to this day such as it was from the beginning, that divine institution would be clearly discerned, and the sweetest harmony would reign in marriage; because the husband would look up with reverence to God; the woman in this would be a faithful assistant to him; and both, with one consent, would cultivate a holy, as well as friendly and peaceful intercourse. Now, it has happened by our fault, and by the corruption of nature, that this happiness of marriage has, in a great measure, perished, or, at least, is mixed and infected with many inconveniences. Hence arise strifes, troubles, sorrows, dissensions, and a boundless sea of evils; and hence it follows, that men are often disturbed by their wives, and suffer through them many discouragements. Still, marriage was not capable of being so far vitiated by the depravity of men, that the blessing which God has once sanctioned by his word should be utterly abolished and extinguished.[5]

The Various Yokes of Submission

Wives, submit yourselves unto your own husbands,
as unto the Lord. - Ephesians 5:22

He comes now to the various conditions of life; for, besides the universal bond of subjection, some are more closely bound to each other, according to their respective callings. The community at large is divided, as it were, into so many yokes, out of which arises mutual obligation. There is, first, the yoke of marriage between husband and wife; - secondly, the yoke which binds parents and children; - and, thirdly, the yoke which connects masters and servants. By this arrangement there are six different classes, for each of whom Paul lays down peculiar duties. He begins with wives, whom he enjoins to be subject to their husbands, in the same manner as to Christ, - as to the Lord. Not that the authority is equal, but wives cannot obey Christ without yielding obedience to their husbands.[6]

Thy Desire Shall Be Unto Thy Husband

Unto the woman he said, I will greatly multiply thy sorrow and thy conception; in sorrow thou shalt bring forth children; and thy desire shall be to thy husband, and he shall rule over thee. - Genesis 3:16

The second punishment which he exacts is subjection. For this form of speech, "Thy desire shall be unto thy husband," is of the same force as if he had said that she should not be free and at her own command, but subject to the authority of her husband and dependent upon his will; or as if he had said, 'Thou shalt desire nothing but what thy husband wishes.' As it is declared afterwards, Unto thee shall be his desire, (Genesis 4:7) Thus the woman, who had perversely exceeded her proper bounds, is forced back to her own position. She had, indeed, previously been subject to her husband, but that was a liberal and gentle subjection; now, however, she is cast into servitude.[7]

Advice To a Young Woman for Her Marriage

There cannot be any doubt but that Sarah was a great solace to our father Abraham, when he had to set forth upon his journey. Follow you her footsteps like one of her daughters, for we see from the example of Lot's wife what is the consequence of looking back. Howsoever that may be, I do entertain the assurance that you have not put a hand to the plough, meaning to look behind and turn back upon it.[8]

Encouragement for a Wife

Wherefore are we not together, to provoke Satan, by meditating upon the things which may well cause us spiritual rejoicing, and give us matter for glorying more than ever, even when we are utterly discomfited according to the world's estimation? ...Above all, understand that now the hour is come when you must shew what a helpmeet you are to Monseigneur your husband, in such a sort that he may always have occasion to bless God, as, he has had hitherto, for having provided him with such a support. I say this, because I consider that it is the principal one that God has left him as regards the creature, without having deprived him of all. I see clearly, though absent, by what zeal you are urged forward to acquit yourself of duty, and what trouble you take to employ yourself therein. For which reason, what I now speak is not so much by way of exhortation as, while congratulating, to uphold you in that good courage which God has given.[9]

Advice To a Wife
Whose Husband Was Captured

If the sorrow which the capture of your husband has caused you has been painful and bitter, I trust nevertheless, that you have in part recognized by the effects which it has produced that God has sent you this affliction only for your good and your spiritual welfare, and this consideration it is which ought to mitigate your distress, and render you patient and submissive to the will of God. For it is consoling to recognize that not only he tries our faith, but also that, in withdrawing us from the allurements and delights of the world which deceive us, he lets us taste his bounty and feel his aid, by gathering us as it were under his wings, that we may say with David that our supreme good is to cleave to him.[10]

For Wives with Unbelieving Husbands

Likewise, ye wives, be in subjection to your own husbands; that, if any obey not the word, they also may without the word be won by the conversation of the wives; While they behold your chaste conversation coupled with fear. - I Peter 3:1-2

He proceeds now to another instance of subjection, and bids wives to be subject to their husbands. And as those seemed to have some pretense for shaking off the yoke, who were united to unbelieving men, he expressly reminds them of their duty, and brings forward a particular reason why they ought the more carefully to obey, even that they might by their probity allure their husbands to the faith. But if wives ought to obey ungodly husbands, with much more promptness ought they to obey, who have believing husbands. But it may seem strange that Peter should say, that a husband might be gained to the Lord without the word; for why is it said, that "faith cometh by hearing" (Romans 10:17)? To this I reply, that Peter's words are not to be so understood as though a holy life alone could lead the unbelieving to Christ, but that it softens and pacifies their minds, so that they might have less dislike to religion; for as bad examples create offenses, so good ones afford no small help. Then Peter shews that wives by a holy and pious life could do so much as to prepare their husbands, without speaking to them on religion, to embrace the faith of Christ.

"While they behold." For minds, however alienated from the true faith, are subdued, when they see the good conduct of believers; for as they understood not the doctrine of Christ, they form an estimate of it by our life. It cannot, then, be but that they will commend Christianity, which teaches purity and fear.[11]

Letter To a Wife with an Unbelieving Husband

But even though you should not know the cause of God's thus dealing with you, it nevertheless becomes you so far to honor him as to deem this point unquestionable; namely, that, since he is all goodness and all justice, we are bound humbly to receive what he sends us, and that there is neither objection nor reply to be made to his dispensations. Exhort yourself then to patience by the word of God, and strive to overcome all temptations, by which I have no doubt you are greatly agitated. In the mean time, pray God continually to convert the heart of your husband, and on your own part make every effort to win him over and fix him in the right path.[12]

Mutual Obligations for Authority and Submission

But if from this you conclude that obedience is to be returned to none but just governors, you reason absurdly. Husbands are bound by mutual duties to their wives, and parents to their children. Should husbands and parents neglect their duty; should the latter be harsh and severe to the children whom they are enjoined not to provoke to anger, and by their severity harass them beyond measure; should the former treat with the greatest contumely the wives whom they are enjoined to love and to spare as the weaker vessels; would children be less bound in duty to their parents, and wives to their husbands? They are made subject to the froward and undutiful. Nay, since the duty of all is not to look behind them, that is, not to inquire into the duties of one another, but to submit each to his own duty, this ought especially to be exemplified in the case of those who are placed under the power of others.[13]

CHAPTER 10

THE PRESERVATION OF MARRIAGE

Abominate Every Form of Lust

H ow do you divorce-proof a marriage? What is the irreducible principle to consider to achieve this goal? Calvin kept his focus on the heart of the matter. He wrote that "nothing in the life of man is more sacred than marriage." With this as the foundation, it is easy to see why he would rail so harshly against whatever would lead to the downfall of a marriage. Calvin understood that the impurity of the heart was the source of the final devastation of the marriage - the sin of adultery. He saw the keeping of the law regarding the adultery of the heart as the secret to preserving marriage.

He also exposed the false doctrine that was popularly held regarding the nature of this sin, noting, "the hypocrisy of the Papists, therefore, is too gross and stupid, when they affirm that lust is not a sin, until it gain the full consent of the heart." Calvin's instruction in the area of adultery can be summarized in the following statement from the *Institutes*, "[Because] God loves chastity and purity, we ought to guard against all uncleanness."

In order to appeal for the preservation of marriage, Calvin clearly identified the various elements of the wrath of God on adulterers because "God, who presides over marriage, will take vengeance on them." He explained the terrible bodily effects of adultery and made it clear that it "covers it with infamy and disgrace." He declared that it was nothing but filthy lust that caused "husbands [to] cast away conjugal love as to those wives whom they have married in their youth."

Calvin's reforms penetrated the common practices of divorce and contradicted the Roman Catholic canon law. While Calvin believed that impious divorce opened men to "pestiferous errors and the foulest delusions," he also maintained that it was lawful in certain circumstances. He wrote, "God chose to make a provision for women who were cruelly oppressed, and for whom it was better that they should at once be set free, than that they should groan beneath a cruel tyranny during their whole lives." This was revolutionary in Calvin's Geneva for it contradicted the common understanding that had been established by the Roman church.

His words are stern warnings for us who live in a time of severe threats to anyone who desires to preserve marriage. We are confronted with rampant virtual adultery through multiple media outlets and are surrounded by a Christian culture which is insensitive to those things which light the fires that burn marriages to the ground.

CALVIN SPEAKS:

The Common Sense of Mankind Declares Adultery to Be Obscene

Thou shalt not commit adultery. - Exodus 20:14

Although one kind of impurity is alone referred to, it is sufficiently plain, from the principle laid down, that believers are generally exhorted to chastity; for, if the Law be a perfect rule of holy living, it would be more than absurd to give a license for fornication, adultery alone being excepted. Furthermore, it is incontrovertible that God will by no means approve or excuse before this tribunal, what the common sense of mankind declares to be obscene; for, although lewdness has everywhere been rampant in every age, still the opinion could never be utterly extinguished, that fornication is a scandal and a sin. Unquestionably what Paul teaches has been prevalently received from the beginning, that a good life consists of three parts, soberness, righteousness, and godliness, (Titus 2:12) and the soberness which he commands differs not from chastity. Besides, when Christ or the Apostles are treating of a perfect life, they always refer believers to the Law; for, as it had been said of old by Moses, "This is the way, walk ye in it"; Christ confirms this, "If thou wilt enter into life, keep the commandments" (Matthew 19:17), and Paul corroborates it, "He that loveth another hath fulfilled the Law," (Romans 13:8) whilst they constantly pronounce a curse against all fornicators. It is not worthwhile to quote the particular passages in which they do so. Now, if Christ and the Apostles, who are the best interpreters of the Law, declare that God's Law is violated no less by fornication than by theft, we assuredly infer, that in this Commandment the whole genus is comprehended under a single species. Wherefore, those have done nothing but betray their disgraceful ignorance, who have sought to be praised for their acuteness on the score of their ridiculous subtlety, when they admitted that fornication is indeed condemned with sufficient clearness and frequency in the New Testament, but not in the Law. For, if they had reasoned justly, inasmuch as God is declared to have blessed marriage, it must at once be concluded, on the contrary, that the connection of male and female, except in marriage, is accursed. This is the argument of the author of the Epistle to the Hebrews, where he contrasts two opposite things; "Marriage (he says) is honorable in all, and the bed undefiled; but whoremongers and adulterers God will judge."[1]

God Loves Chastity and Purity

The purport of this commandment is, that as God loves chastity and purity, we ought to guard against all uncleanness. The substance of the commandment therefore is, that we must not defile ourselves with any impurity or libidinous excess. To this corresponds the affirmative, that we must regulate every part of our conduct chastely and continently. The thing expressly forbidden is adultery, to which lust naturally tends, that its filthiness (being of a grosser and more palpable form, in as much as it casts a stain even on the body) may dispose us to abominate every form of lust. As the law under which man was created was not to lead a life of solitude, but enjoy a help meet for him, and ever since he fell under the curse the necessity for this mode of life is increased; the Lord made the requisite provision for us in this respect by the institution of marriage, which, entered into under his authority, he has also sanctified with his blessing. Hence, it is evident, that any mode of cohabitation different from marriage is cursed in his sight, and that the conjugal relation was ordained as a necessary means of preventing us from giving way to unbridled lust.[2]

The design of the Seventh Commandment is, that, because God loves purity, we ought to put away from us all uncleanness. He therefore forbids adultery in mind, word, and deed.[3]

Understanding Adultery of the Heart - How to Avoid Being Dull and Stupid in Judging Our Sins

Ye have heard that it was said by them of old time, Thou shalt not commit adultery: But I say unto you, That whosoever looketh on a woman to lust after her hath committed adultery with her already in his heart. - Matthew 5:27-28

Christ proceeds with his subject, and shows, that the law of God not only has authority over the life, in a political view, to form the outward manners, but that it requires pure and holy affections of the heart. We must remember what I have already stated, that though Christ quotes the very words of the law, it is the gross and false meaning, which had been put upon it by dishonest interpreters, that he blames. He has already told us, that he did not come as a new Legislator, but as the faithful expounder of a law which had been already given. It might be objected that, through long practice, that interpretation had grown old. Christ expressly admits this, but meets it by saying, that the antiquity of an error ought not to be allowed to plead in its favor.

"Whoever shall look upon a woman." *The design of Christ was to condemn generally the lust of the flesh. He says, that not only those who have seduced their neighbors' wives, but those who have polluted their eyes by an immodest look, are adulterers before God. This is a synecdoche, for not only the eyes, but even the concealed flames of the heart, render men guilty of adultery. Accordingly, Paul makes chastity (1 Corinthians 7:34) to consist both in body and in mind. But Christ reckoned it enough to refute the gross mistake which was prevalent; for they thought that it was only necessary to guard against outward adultery. As it is generally by the wantonness of the eyes that temptations are presented to the mind, and as lust enters, as it were, by that door, Christ used this mode of speaking, when he wished to condemn lust, which is evident from the expression, to lust after her. This teaches us also, that not only those who form a deliberate purpose of fornication, but those who admit any polluted thoughts, are reckoned adulterers before God. The hypocrisy of the Papists, therefore, is too gross and stupid, when they affirm that lust is not a sin, until it gain the full consent of the heart. But we need not wonder that they make sin to be so small a matter: for those who ascribe righteousness to the merit of works must be very dull and stupid in judging of their sins.*[4]

The Heart of Adultery

The Pharisees having instilled into the people the erroneous idea that the Law was fulfilled by everyone who did not in external act do anything against the Law, he pronounces this a most dangerous delusion, and declares that an immodest look is adultery, and that hatred of a brother is murder... Having forbidden us to turn and incline our mind to wrath, hatred, adultery, theft, and falsehood, he now forbids us to give our thoughts the same direction.[5]

The Eyes Are As Torches to Inflame the Heart to Lust

And he left all that he had in Joseph's hand; and he knew not ought he had, save the bread which he did eat. And Joseph was a goodly person, and well favoured. - Genesis 39:6

When it is said that Potiphar's wife "cast her eyes upon Joseph," the Holy Spirit, by this form of speech, admonishes all women, that if they have chastity in their heart, they must guard it by modesty of demeanor. For, on this account also, they bear a veil upon their heads, that they may restrain themselves from every sinful allurement: not that it is wrong for a woman to look at men; but Moses here describes an impure and dissolute look. She had often before looked upon Joseph without sin: but now, for the first time, she casts her eyes upon him,

CHAPTER 10: THE PRESERVATION OF MARRIAGE

and contemplates his beauty more boldly and wantonly than became a modest woman. Thus we see that the eyes were as torches to inflame the heart to lust.[6]

A Severe Warning To Adulterers

But God came to Abimelech in a dream by night, and said to him, Behold, thou art but a dead man, for the woman which thou hast taken; for she is a man's wife. - Genesis 20:3

Although God reproved King Abimelech, for the sake of Abraham, whom he covered with his special protection; he yet intends to show, generally, his high displeasure against adultery. And, in truth, here is no express mention of Abraham; but rather a general announcement is made, for the purpose of maintaining conjugal fidelity. 'Thou shalt die, because thou hast seized upon a women who was joined to a husband.' Let us therefore learn, that a precept was given in these words, to mankind, which forbids any one to touch his neighbor's wife. And, truly, since nothing in the life of man is more sacred than marriage, it is not to be wondered at, that the Lord should require mutual fidelity to be cherished between husbands and wives and should declare that he will be the Avenger of it, as often as it is violated. He now addresses himself, indeed, only to one man; but the warning ought to sound in the ears of all, that adulterers - although they may exult with impunity for a time - shall yet feel that God, who presides over marriage, will take vengeance on them.[7]

Bridle All Lusts

*Not in the lust of concupiscence, even as the Gentiles
which know not God.* - 1 Thessalonians 4:5

*By the lust of concupiscence, he means all base lusts of the
flesh, but, at the same time, by this manner of expression,
he brands with dishonor all desires that allure us to
pleasure and carnal delights, as in Romans 13:14, he bids
us have no care for the flesh in respect of the lust thereof.
For when men give indulgence to their appetites, there
are no bounds to lasciviousness. Hence the only means of
maintaining temperance is to bridle all lusts. As for the
expression, that every one of you may know to possess his
vessel, some explain it as referring to a wife, as though it
had been said, "Let husbands dwell with their wives in all
chastity." As, however, he addresses husbands and wives
indiscriminately, there can be no doubt that he employs the
term vessel to mean body. For every one has his body as a
house, as it were, in which he dwells. He would, therefore,
have us keep our body pure from all uncleanness. And
honor, that is, honorably, for the man that prostitutes his
body to fornication, covers it with infamy and disgrace.*[8]

Wrong Done To a Young Wife

Yet ye say, Wherefore? Because the LORD hath been witness between thee and the wife of thy youth, against whom thou hast dealt treacherously: yet is she thy companion, and the wife of thy covenant. - Malachi 2:14

He calls her the wife of his youth, because the more filthy is the lust when husbands cast away conjugal love as to those wives whom they have married in their youth. The bond of marriage is indeed in all cases inviolable, even between the old, but it is a circumstance which increases the turpitude of the deed, when any one alienates himself from a wife whom he married when a girl and in the flower of her age: for youth conciliates love; and we also see that when a husband and his wife have lived together for many years, mutual love prevails between them to extreme old age, because their hearts were united together in their youth. It is not then without reason that this circumstance is mentioned, for the lust of the priests was the more filthy and as it were the more monstrous, because they forsook wives whom they ought to have regarded with the tenderest love, as they had married them when they were young: Thou hast dealt unfaithfully with her, he says, though she was thy consort and the wife of thy covenant".[9]

The Slippery Slope of Lust While Young

And Shechem spake unto his father Hamor, saying,
Get me this damsel to wife. - Genesis 34:4

In this place it is more clearly expressed, that Shechem desired to have Dinah for his wife; for his lust was not so unbridled, that when he had defiled, he despised her. Besides, a laudable modesty is shown, since he pays deference to the will of his father; for he does not attempt to form a contract of marriage of his own mind, but leaves this to his father's authority. For though he had basely fallen through the precipitate ardor of lust, yet now returning to himself, he follows the guidance of nature. So much the more ought young men to take heed to themselves, lest in the slippery period of their age, the lusts of the flesh should impel them to many crimes. For, at this day, greater license everywhere prevails, so that no moderation restrains youths from shameful conduct.[10]

Why Divorce Is Repugnant and Abolishes What God Has Joined Together

When a man hath taken a wife, and married her, and it come to pass that she find no favour in his eyes, because he hath found some uncleanness in her: then let him write her a bill of divorcement, and give it in her hand, and send her out of his house. - Deuteronomy 24:1

Although what relates to divorce was granted in indulgence to the Jews, yet Christ pronounces that it was never in accordance with the Law, because it is directly repugnant to the first institution of God, from whence a perpetual and inviolable rule is to be sought. It is proverbially said that the laws of nature are indissoluble; and God has declared once for all, that the bond of union between husband and wife is closer than that of parent and child; wherefore, if a son cannot shake off the paternal yoke, no cause can permit the dissolution of the connection which a man has with his wife. Hence it appears how great was the perverseness of that nation, which could not be restrained from dissolving a most sacred and inviolable tie. Meanwhile the Jews improperly concluded from their impunity that that was lawful, which God did not punish because of the hardness of their hearts; whereas they ought rather to have considered, agreeably to the answer of Christ, that man is not at liberty to separate those whom God hath joined together. (Matthew 19:6) Still, God chose to make a provision for women who were cruelly oppressed, and for whom it was better that they should at once be set free, than that they should groan beneath a cruel tyranny during their whole lives. Thus, in Malachi, divorce is preferred to polygamy, since it would be a more tolerable condition to be divorced than to bear with a harlot and a rival (Malachi 2:14). And undoubtedly the bill or scroll of divorce, whilst it cleared the woman from all disgrace, cast some reproach on the husband, for he who confesses that he puts away his wife, because she does not please him, brings himself under the accusation both of moroseness and inconstancy. For what gross levity and disgraceful inconstancy it shows, that a husband should be so offended with some imperfection or disease in his wife, as to cast away from him half of himself! We see, then, that husbands were indirectly condemned by the writing of divorce, since they thus committed an injury against their wives who were chaste, and in other respects what they should be. On these grounds, God in Isaiah, in order that He might take away from the Jews all subject of complaint, bids them produce the bill of divorce, if He had given any to their mother, (Isaiah 1:1) as much as to say, that His cause for rejecting them was just, because they had treacherously revolted to ungodliness.

Some interpreters do not read these three verses continuously, but suppose the sense to be complete at the end of the first, wherein the husband testifies that he divorces his wife for no offense, but because her beauty does not satisfy his lust. If, however, we give more close attention, we shall see that it is only one provision of the Law, viz., that when a man has divorced his wife, it is not lawful for him to marry her again if she have married another. The reason of the law is, that, by prostituting his wife, he would be, as far as in him lay, acting like a procurer. In this view, it is said that she was defiled, because he had contaminated her body, for the liberty which he gave her could not abolish the first institution of God, but rather, as Christ teaches, gave cause for adultery (Matthew 5:31; 19:9). Thus, the Israelites were reminded that, although they divorced their wives with impunity, still this license was by no means excused before God.[11]

How Wives Are "Miserably Tormented"

For the LORD, the God of Israel, saith that he hateth putting away: for one covereth violence with his garment, saith the LORD of hosts: therefore take heed to your spirit, that ye deal not treacherously. - Malachi 2:16

But if a comparison be made, Malachi says, that it is a lighter crime to dismiss a wife than to marry many wives. We hence learn how abominable polygamy is in the sight of God. I do not consider polygamy to be what the foolish Papists have made it, who call not those polygamists who have many wives at the same time, but those who marry another when the former one is dead. This is gross ignorance. Polygamy, properly so called, is when a person takes many wives, as it was commonly done in the East: and those nations, we know, have always been libidinous, and never observe the marriage vow. As then their lasciviousness was so great that they were like brute beasts, every one married several wives; and this abuse continues at this day among the Turks and the Persian and other nations. Here, however, where God compares polygamy with divorce, he says that polygamy is the worse and more detestable crime; for the husband impurely connects himself with another woman, and then, not only deals unfaithfully with his wife to whom he is bound, but also forcibly detains her: thus his crime is doubled. For if he replies and says that he keeps the wife to whom he is bound, he is yet an adulterer as to the second wife: thus he blends, as they say, holy with profane things; and then to adultery and lasciviousness he adds cruelty, for he holds under his authority a miserable woman, who would prefer death to such a condition, for we know what power jealousy has over women. And when any one introduces a harlot, how can a lawful wife bear such an indignity without being miserably tormented?[12]

Christ on Divorce -
Tearing the Body in Pieces

The Pharisees also came unto him, tempting him, and saying unto him, Is it lawful for a man to put away his wife for every cause? And he answered and said unto them, Have ye not read, that he which made them at the beginning made them male and female? - Matthew 19:3-4

Though the Pharisees lay snares for Christ, and cunningly endeavor to impose upon him, yet their malice proves to be highly useful to us, as the Lord knows how to turn, in a wonderful manner, to the advantage of his people all the contrivances of wicked men to overthrow sound doctrine.

For, by means of this occurrence, a question arising out of the liberty of divorce was settled, and a fixed law was laid down as to the sacred and indissoluble bond of marriage. The occasion of this quibbling was, that the reply, in whatever way it were given, could not, as they thought, fail to be offensive.

They ask, Is it lawful for a man to divorce his wife for any cause whatever? If Christ reply in the negative, they will exclaim that he wickedly abolishes the Law; and if in the affirmative, they will give out that he is not a prophet of God, but rather a pander, who lends such countenance to the lust of men. Such were the calculations which they had made in their own minds; but the Son of God, who knew how to take the wise in their own craftiness (Job 5:13), disappointed them, sternly opposing unlawful divorces, and at the same time showing that he brings forward nothing which is inconsistent with the Law. For he includes the whole question under two heads: that the order of creation ought to serve for a law, that the husband should maintain conjugal fidelity during the whole of life; and that divorces were permitted, not because they were lawful, but because Moses had to deal with a rebellious and intractable nation.

Have you not read? Christ does not indeed reply directly to what was asked, but he fully meets the question which was proposed; just as if a person now interrogated about the Mass were to explain faithfully the mystery of the Holy Supper, and at length to conclude, that they are guilty of sacrilege and forgery who venture either to add or to take away anything from the pure institution of the Lord, he would plainly overturn the pretended sacrifice of the Mass. Now Christ assumes as an admitted principle, that at the beginning God joined the male to the female, so that the two made an entire man; and therefore he who divorces his wife tears from him, as it were, the half of himself. But nature does not allow any man to tear in pieces his own body.

He adds another argument drawn from the less to the greater. The bond of marriage is more sacred than that which binds children to their parents. But piety binds children to their parents by a link which cannot be broken. Much less then can the husband renounce his wife. Hence it follows, that a chain which God made is burst asunder, if the husband divorce his wife.

Now the meaning of the words is this: God, who created the human race, made them male and female, so that every man might be satisfied with his own wife, and might not desire more...And thus from the order of creation is proved the inviolable union of one husband with one wife.[13]

Impious Divorce Brings Just Punishment

But since as much as in them lies they loose or burst the sacred bond of unity, none of them escapes the just punishment of this impious divorce, but become fascinated with pestiferous errors, and the foulest delusions. Wherefore, in order that the pure simplicity of the faith may flourish among us, let us not decline to use this exercise of piety, which God by his institution of it has shown to be necessary, and which he so highly recommends.[14]

Polygamy is Perverse and Degenerate

And Lamech took unto him two wives: the name of the one was Adah, and the name of the other Zillah. - Genesis 4:19

We have here the origin of polygamy in a perverse and degenerate race; and the first author of it, a cruel man, destitute of all humanity. Whether he had been impelled by an immoderate desire of augmenting his own family, as proud and ambitious men are wont to be, or by mere lust, it is of little consequence to determine, because, in either way he violated the sacred law of marriage, which had been delivered by God. For God had determined, that "they" "two should be one flesh," and that is the perpetual order of nature. Lamech, with brutal contempt of God, corrupts nature's laws. The Lord, therefore, willed that the corruption of lawful marriage should proceed from the house of Cain, and from the person of Lamech, in order that polygamists might be ashamed of the example.[15]

CHAPTER 11

THE BLESSING OF CHILDREN

Children – The Singular Kindness of God

*C*ultures rise and fall on their treatment of children. With Calvin, God's words and acts regarding children caused an upwelling of gratitude - for children were gifts and blessings of God. As he contemplated the blessings of children, he extolled God's wisdom for creating them and chastised man for his blindness in missing their importance. He pointed out that unless men viewed children as gifts of God, they would be "careless and reluctant in providing for their support." He speaks of them as "earthly blessings," and reminds us that children are "a treasure... granted by God." His high view of children caused him to urge parents to "celebrate the singular kindness of God, in their offspring."

CALVIN SPEAKS:

Children Are a Treasure

For in reality it is great baseness when a treasure, such as children are, is granted by God, so soon as it has been bestowed to pollute it with the superstitions which men have mixed up with the holy ordinance of baptism. But since this sacrament is a solemn reception into the church of God, or rather a testimony of burghership in the heavenly city into which are enrolled all those whom God adopts for his children, above all things it is to be observed that it is not lawful to administer it except in the society of professed believers.[1]

Celebrating the Kindness of God in Giving Offspring

And he lifted up his eyes, and saw the women and the children; and said, Who are those with thee? And he said, The children which God hath graciously given thy servant. - Genesis 33:5

Moses relates the conversation held between the brothers. And as Esau had testified his fraternal affection by tears and embraces, there is no doubt that he inquires after the children in a spirit of congratulation. The answer of Jacob breathes piety as well as modesty; for when he replies, that his numerous seed had been given him by God, he acknowledges and confesses that children are not so produced by nature as to subvert the truth of the declaration, that the fruit of the womb is a reward and gift of God. And truly, since the fecundity of brute animals is the gift of God, how much more is this the case with men, who are created after his own image. Let parents then learn to consider, and to celebrate the singular kindness of God, in their offspring.[2]

Polluting Children with Religious Superstitions

Now, on the contrary, as one of the articles of our complaint was, that he blamed me for having written that fathers polluted their children, in presenting them to the superstitions which are prevalent in Popery, we alleged proofs of our opinion that ought to have more than satisfied him, viz., that the name of God, his temple, and the sacraments are certainly polluted by those who make a bad use of them, and just as the father sanctifies his child, in dedicating it to God, so he defiles it, in prostituting it to superstitions that ought to be condemned. He, like a *doctor of the highest grade, "These then are your reasons; I think differently." Here I could not avoid saying to him: "I believe, M. de la Vau, I might be thought to have almost as much authority as you to allege what I think, or my private opinion, but God forbid that I should give such loose to my fantasies; and moreover the question here is not about what one weens or overweens, but simply to stand by what God points out to us.*[3]

Children: Heritage and Reward

Lo, children are an heritage of the LORD: and the fruit of the womb is his reward. As arrows are in the hand of a mighty man; so are children of the youth. Happy is the man that hath his quiver full of them: they shall not be ashamed, but they shall speak with the enemies in the gate. - Psalm 127:3-5

Solomon calls children the heritage of God, and the fruit of the womb his gift; for the Hebrew word, sachar, translated reward, signifies whatever benefits God bestows upon men, as is plainly manifest from many passages of Scripture. The meaning then is, that, children are not the fruit of chance, but that God, as it seems good to him, distributes to every man his share of them. Moreover, as the Prophet repeats the same thing twice, heritage and reward are to be understood as equivalent; for both these terms are set in opposition to fortune, or the strength of men. The stronger a man is he seems so much the better fitted for procreation. Solomon declares on the contrary, that those become fathers to whom God vouchsafes that honor. As the majority of children are not always a source of joy to their parents, a second favor of God is added, which is his forming the minds of children, and adorning them with an excellent disposition, and all kinds of virtues. Aristotle in his Politics very properly discusses the question whether poluteknia, that is, the having of many children, ought to be accounted among good things or no; and he decides it in the negative, unless there is added eujgeneia, that is, generosity or goodness of nature in the children themselves. And assuredly it would be a far happier lot for many to be without children, or barren, than to have a numerous offspring, proving to them only the cause of tears and groans. In order, then, to set forth this blessing of God - the having offspring - in a clear light, Solomon commends a virtuous and generous disposition in children.[4]

Through Children Men Are Defended

The similitude introduced for this purpose is, that as an archer is armed 'with a well furnished bow,' so men are defended by their children, as it were with a bow and all arrow. This similitude might seem, at first sight, a little too harsh; but if it is examined somewhat more closely, its elegance will be readily admitted. The Prophet means that

*those who are without children are in a manner unarmed;
for what else is it to be childless but to be solitary? It is
no small gift of God for a man to be renewed in his
posterity; for God then gives him new strength, that he
who otherwise would straightway decay, may begin as it
were to live a second time. The knowledge of this doctrine
is highly useful. The fruitfulness even of the lower animals
is expressly ascribed to God alone; and if he would have
it to be accounted his benefit that kine, and sheep, and
mares conceive, how inexcusable will be the impiety of
men, if when he adorns them with the honorable title of
fathers, they account this favor as nothing. It is also to be
added, that unless men regard their children as the gift
of God, they are careless and reluctant in providing for
their support, just as on the other hand this knowledge
contributes in a very eminent degree to encourage them in
bringing up their offspring. Farther, he who thus reflects
upon the goodness of God in giving him children, will
readily and with a settled mind look for the continuance
of God's grace; and although he may have but a small
inheritance to leave them, he will not be unduly careful on
that account.*[5]

How Children Shut the Mouths
of the Malevolent

Here Solomon describes such children as, distinguished by uprightness and integrity, have no hesitation in rendering an account of their life, that they may shut the mouths of the malevolent and of calumniators. In ancient times, as is well known, judicial assemblies were held at the gates of cities. He therefore here speaks of the gate, as if in the present day one should speak of the bench, or the courts, or the senate. Let it be observed that what is chiefly praised in children is innocence, that fathers may estimate this grace at its true value. In the preceding clause he had compared children endued with virtue and excellence of nature to arrows. Now, that no man may put a violent construction upon this comparison, as if it were intended to give children leave, like robbers, to rush upon doing mischief to such as come in their way, reckless of right and wrong, he expressly represents virtue and moral integrity as constituting the protection which they ought to afford to their fathers. He teaches us, then, that the children which we ought to wish for, are not such as may violently oppress the wretched and suffering, or overreach others by craft and deceit, or accumulate great riches by unlawful means, or acquire for themselves tyrannical authority, but such as will practice uprightness, and be willing to live in obedience to the laws, and prepared to render an account of their life. Farther, although fathers ought diligently to form their children under a system of holy discipline, yet let them remember that they will never succeed in attaining the object aimed at, save by the pure and special grace of God. Solomon also tacitly intimates that however zealously we may be devoted to the practice of integrity, we shall never be without detractors and slanderers; for if integrity of life were exempt from all calumny, we would have no quarrel with our enemies. [6]

In Praise of Fertility

Thus hath the Lord dealt with me in the days wherein he looked on me, to take away my reproach among men. - Luke 1:25

She extols in private the goodness of God, until the time is fully come for making it generally known. There is reason to believe that her husband had informed her by writing of the promised offspring, in consequence of which she affirms with greater certainty and freedom that God was the author of this favor. This is confirmed by the following words, when he looked, that he might take away my reproach; for she assigns it as the cause of her barrenness that the favor of God had been at that time withdrawn from her. Among earthly blessings, Scripture speaks in the highest terms of the gift of offspring. And justly: for, if the productiveness of the inferior animals is his blessing, the increase and fruitfulness of the human race ought to be reckoned a much higher favor. It is no small or mean honor, that God, who alone is entitled to be regarded as a Father, admits the children of the dust to share with him this title. Let us, therefore, hold this doctrine, that "children are an heritage of the Lord, and the fruit of the womb is his reward" (Psalm 127:3). But Elisabeth looked farther, for, though barren and old, she had conceived by a remarkable miracle, and contrary to the ordinary course of nature.[7]

Childbearing - a Heroic Virtue

Notwithstanding she shall be saved in childbearing, if they continue in faith and charity and holiness with sobriety. - I Timothy 2:15

Through child-bearing. To censorious men it might appear absurd, for an Apostle of Christ not only to exhort women to give attention to the birth of offspring, but to press this work as religious and holy to such an extent as to represent it in the light of the means of procuring salvation. Nay, we even see with what reproaches the conjugal bed has been slandered by hypocrites, who wished to be thought more holy than all other men. But there is no difficulty in replying to these sneers of the ungodly. First, here the Apostle does not speak merely about having children, but about enduring all the distresses, which are manifold and severe, both in the birth and in the rearing of children. Secondly, whatever hypocrites or wise men of the world may think of it, when a woman, considering to what she has been called, submits to the condition which God has assigned to her, and does not refuse to endure the pains, or rather the fearful anguish, of parturition, or anxiety about her offspring, or anything else that belongs to her duty, God values this obedience more highly than if, in some other manner, she made a great display of heroic virtues, while she refused to obey the calling of God. To this must be added, that no consolation could be more appropriate or more efficacious than to shew that the very means (so to speak) of procuring salvation are found in the punishment itself.[8]

CHAPTER 12

THE SALVATION OF CHILDREN

Corruption Commencing in Adam, is, by Perpetual Descent

U nderstanding the nature of children and the means of their salvation was vital to Calvin. Most critical for him was an awareness of original sin and the destitute nature of the soul without Christ. Calvin understood that in our ministry to children, helping them to know their true condition and their need for Christ was paramount. Calvin recognized the virtues of parents who provide a healthy home environment and the impact that godliness could have on their children, but he also maintained that that this "does not prevent the primary and universal curse." He upheld the doctrine of original sin, declaring that "from a corrupt root corrupt branches [proceed, transmitting] their corruption to the saplings which spring from them."

CALVIN SPEAKS:

Corruption of Sin Passed On To Children

To the understanding of this subject, there is no necessity for an anxious discussion (which in no small degree perplexed the ancient doctors), as to whether the soul of the child comes by transmission from the soul of the parent. It should be enough for us to know that Adam was made the depository of the endowments which God was pleased to bestow on human nature, and that, therefore, when he lost what he had received, he lost not only for himself but for us all. ...There is nothing absurd, therefore, in the view, that when he was divested, his nature was left naked and destitute that he having been defiled by sin, the pollution extends to all his seed. Thus, from a corrupt root corrupt branches proceeding, transmit their corruption to the saplings which spring from them. The children being vitiated in their parents, conveyed the taint to the grandchildren; in other words, corruption commencing in Adam, is, by perpetual descent, conveyed from those preceding to those coming after them. The cause of the contagion is neither in the substance of the flesh nor the soul, but God was pleased to ordain that those gifts which he had bestowed on the first man, that man should lose as well for his descendants as for himself. The Pelagian cavil, as to the improbability of children deriving corruption from pious parents, whereas, they ought rather to be sanctified by their purity, is easily refuted... Moreover, though godly parents do in some measure contribute to the holiness of their offspring, this is by the blessing of God; a blessing, however, which does not prevent the primary and universal curse of the whole race from previously taking effect. Guilt is from nature, whereas sanctification is from supernatural grace.[1]

Children - Born Defiled by Sin's Stains

That is, they have been enveloped in original sin and defiled by its stains. For that reason, even infants themselves, while they carry their condemnation along with them from the mother's womb, are guilty not of another's fault but of their own. For, even though the fruits of their iniquity have not yet come forth, they have the seed enclosed within them. Indeed, their whole nature is a seed of sin; hence it can be only hateful and abhorrent to God. From this it follows that it is rightly considered sin in God's sight, for without guilt there would be no accusation.[2]

CHAPTER 13

THE FATHER'S DISCIPLESHIP OF CHILDREN

Diligent and Assiduous Teaching

C alvin recognized the supreme importance of the father's role in the discipleship of children. Not only was this achieved by the diligence of fathers but also by "the ineffable kindness of God" in turning the hearts of fathers to their children that "restored from discord to unity so as to become united in one faith." In contrast to our own age where parents are content to systematically outsource their children's education, Calvin knew that it was the primary responsibility of the home. He said, "It is the duty of parents to apply themselves diligently to the work of communicating what they have learned from the Lord to their children." This instruction was not something that could be hit and miss, rather, "they should be diligent and assiduous in teaching their children" that "they might celebrate the praises of Jehovah, in the wonderful works which he hath done." He maintained that fathers did not have the option to keep to themselves, and that "no one may retain his knowledge for his own private use; but that each may edify others."

He warned of the trans-generational impact of child raising, recognizing that diligence must be given to raising children "in order that the truth of God, which is eternal, may live and flourish after our death; and that thus, when we are dead, a holy course of living may survive and remain." Thus, he argued that the teaching of children was of enormous importance and urged that parents "take measures for having them brought up betimes in his fear."

As noted in the previous section, Calvin believed that the doctrine of original sin was true. This reality makes the diligent raising of children in the fear of the Lord vitally necessary, for children left to themselves will bring their mothers shame (Proverbs 29:15). At the same time, he maintained that children should "be fondly cherished" and brought up with gentleness and patience, thus finding the divine balance between the rod and the staff.

CALVIN SPEAKS:

Fathers and Children Restored from Discord To Unity

And he shall turn the heart of the fathers to the children, and the heart of the children to their fathers, lest I come and smite the earth with a curse. - Malachi 4:6

By saying that he would turn the hearts of fathers to sons and of sons to fathers, He points out not a simple union or consent, for men often unite together, and yet God reprobates and hates their union; but the Prophet here has in view the origin of the people, even Abraham and other holy patriarchs. Had he spoken of the Egyptians or the Assyrians, or some other nations, this turning would not have been so wonderful; but when he speaks of the holy and chosen race, it is no wonder that he mentions it as an instance of the ineffable kindness of God, that they were all to be gathered and restored from discord to unity, so as to become united in one faith.[1]

Advice for a Parent on the Greatest Benefit That Can Be Granted To Children

It is certain that nothing whatever ought to hinder us from the discharge of what is due to our heavenly Father, and to that kind Redeemer whom he has sent to us; but the better the opportunity of each, so much the more guilty does he become if he does not the more readily discharge his duty. I am well aware that you have regard to your children, and I do not say but that this is right, provided that the sovereign Father of both you and them be not left out. But consider that the greatest benefit which you can confer upon them, is to shew them the way to follow God.[2]

A Fatherhood That Transmits Doctrine To Children

For I know him, that he will command his children and his household after him, and they shall keep the way of the LORD, to do justice and judgment; that the LORD may bring upon Abraham that which he hath spoken of him. - Genesis 18:19

And truly, God does not make known his will to us, that the knowledge of it may perish with us, but that we may be his witnesses to posterity and that they may deliver the knowledge received through us, from hand to hand (as we say), to their descendants. Wherefore, it is the duty of parents to apply themselves diligently to the work of communicating what they have learned from the Lord to their children. In this manner the truth of God is to be propagated by us, so that no one may retain his knowledge for his own private use; but that each may edify others, according to his own calling, and to the measure of his faith. There is however no doubt, that the gross ignorance which reigns in the world, is the just punishment of men's idleness. For whereas the greater part close their eyes to the offered light of heavenly doctrine; yet there are those who stifle it, by not taking care to transmit it to their children. The Lord therefore righteously takes away the precious treasure of his word, to punish the world for its sloth. The expression after him is also to be noticed; by which we are taught that we must not only take care of our families, to govern them duly, while we live; but that we must give diligence, in order that the truth of God, which is eternal, may live and flourish after our death; and that thus, when we are dead, a holy course of living may survive and remain.[3]

Fathers - Diligent and Assiduous in Teaching Their Children

And that thou mayest tell in the ears of thy son, and of thy son's son, what things I have wrought in Egypt, and my signs which I have done among them; that ye may know how that I am the LORD. - Exodus 10:2

It was proper, then, that their posterity should be thus instructed by their fathers, that they might have no doubts as to the author of so illustrious a work. But it is here required of the fathers, who had been eye-witnesses of the signs, that they should be diligent and assiduous in teaching their children; and on these also, care and attention in learning is enjoined, that the recollection of God's mercies should flourish throughout all ages. The practical effect of this doctrine is seen in Psalms 44 and Psalm 105.[4]

The Knowledge of God Published from Age To Age Without Interruption

We will not hide them from their children, shewing to the generation to come the praises of the LORD, and his strength, and his wonderful works that he hath done. - Psalm 78:4

Some take the verb nechached, in the nephil conjugation, and translate it, they are not concealed or hidden. But it ought, according to the rules of grammar, to be resolved thus: We will not conceal them from our posterity, implying, that what we have been taught by our ancestors we should endeavor to transmit to their children. By this means, all pretense of ignorance is removed, for it was the will of God that these things should be published from age to age without interruption; so that being transmitted from father to child in each family, they might reach even the last family of man. The end for which this was to be done is shown - that they might celebrate the praises of Jehovah, in the wonderful works which he hath done.[5]

CHAPTER 14

CATECHIZING CHILDREN

That All Would Have Some Methodical Instruction

A long with many other reformers and their Puritan successors, Calvin was a famous advocate of catechisms. He took his pattern from the ancient church where at adolescence "a child often would present himself to the church to declare his confession of faith, would be examined in each article." In doing so, children would "discern the difference" between truth and falsehood. He wanted to establish a "common formula of instruction for little children and for ignorant persons." He had confidence that this would "build an edifice of long duration," protect him from believing false doctrine and help him "profit from what shall be preached." Calvin provided 372 catechism questions in his 1560 children's catechism, "A Dialogue Between the Minister and the Child."

CALVIN SPEAKS:

The Importance of Catechisms for Children

Next, that they have a common formula of instruction for little children and for ignorant persons, serving to make them familiar with sound doctrine, so that they may be able to discern the difference between it and the falsehood and corruptions which may be brought forward in opposition to it. Believe me, Monseigneur, the Church of God will never preserve itself without a Catechism, for it is like the seed to keep the good grain from dying out, and causing it to multiply from age to age. And therefore, if you desire to build an edifice which shall be of long duration, and which shall not soon fall into decay, make provision for the children being instructed in a good Catechism, which may shew them briefly, and in language level to their tender age, wherein true Christianity consists. This Catechism will serve two purposes, to wit, as an introduction to the whole people, so that everyone may profit from what shall be preached, and also to enable them to discern when any presumptuous person puts forward strange doctrine.[1]

Catechizing Children - To Arouse Slothful Parents

How I wish that we might have kept the custom which, as I have said, existed among the ancient Christians before this misborn wraith of a sacrament came to birth! Not that it would be a confirmation such as they fancy, which cannot be named without doing injustice to baptism; but a catechizing, in which children or those near adolescence would give an account of their faith before the church. But the best method of catechizing would be to have a manual drafted for this exercise, containing and summarizing in simple manner most of the articles of our religion, on which the whole believers' church ought to agree without controversy. A child often would present himself to the church to declare his confession of faith, would be examined in each article, and answer to each; if he were ignorant of anything or insufficiently understood it, he would be taught. Thus, while the church looks on as a witness, he would profess the one true and sincere faith, in which the believing folk with one mind worship the one God. If this discipline were in effect today, it would certainly arouse some slothful parents, who carelessly neglect the instruction of their children as a matter of no concern to them, for then they could not overlook it without public disgrace. There would be greater agreement in faith among Christian people, and not so many would go untaught and ignorant; some would not be so rashly carried away with new and strange doctrines; in short, all would have some methodical instruction, so to speak, in Christian doctrine.[2]

CHAPTER 15

THE DISCIPLINE
OF CHILDREN

*Increase the Cheerfulness and
Activity of their Obedience*

C alvin believed that parents were responsible for the
discipline of children. He taught that they will "render
an account, when any evil shall be committed in their family."
He was an advocate of stern discipline, but he also exhorted
parents "not to irritate their children by unreasonable severity,"
because it "would excite hatred, and would lead them to throw
off the yoke altogether." He exposed the mistake that many
parents make in the midst of their discipline, to forget "gentleness
and forbearance." And he made sure to encourage that they be
"mild and considerate." Further, he commented on the heart of
the parents. He said that child discipline should be marked by
parents who "draw nearer to Jesus Christ, and know him more
intimately."

CALVIN SPEAKS:

Severity of Correction for Children Required

For unless fathers use severity and correction when need requireth, when they see their children to be so wicked they are guilty, inasmuch as they fail in doing their duty. Our Lord hath given them authority over their houses and offspring. And wherefore, unless it be to the end to keep them in awe and to restrain them, that they may render an account, when any evil shall be committed in their family?[1]

Unreasonable Severity or Kind Liberal Treatment

And, ye fathers, provoke not your children to wrath: but bring them up in the nurture and admonition of the Lord. - Ephesians 6:4

Parents, on the other hand, are exhorted not to irritate their children by unreasonable severity. This would excite hatred, and would lead them to throw off the yoke altogether. Accordingly, in writing to the Colossians, he adds, "lest they be discouraged" (Colossians 3:21). Kind and liberal treatment has rather a tendency to cherish reverence for their parents, and to, while a harsh and unkind manner rouses them to obstinacy, and destroys the natural affections. But Paul goes on to say, "let them be fondly cherished;" for the Greek word, ἐκτρέφετε, which is translated bring up, unquestionably conveys the idea of gentleness and forbearance. To guard them, however, against the opposite and frequent evil of excessive indulgence, he again draws the rein which he had slackened, and adds, in the instruction and reproof of the Lord. It is not the will of God that parents, in the exercise of kindness, shall spare and corrupt their children. Let their conduct towards their children be at once mild and considerate, so as to guide them in the fear of the Lord, and correct them also when they go astray. That age is so apt to become wanton, that it requires frequent admonition and restraint.[2]

The Heart of a Parent - Drawing Nearer To Christ

Whereby the apostle means that in proportion as we draw nearer to Jesus Christ, and know him more intimately, the grace and virtue of his Spirit will at the same time grow and be multiplied in us. So then be it your constant care to profit more and more. And besides all that, you *have to think of your children, whom God has confided to your charge for this end, that they should be dedicated to him, and that he should be the supreme Father of them as of you. It is true that many persons are prevented from discharging their duties towards their children, because their single desire is to further the advancement of their offspring in the world. But this is a pitiful and perverse consideration. I entreat you then since God has bestowed on you a race of children gifted, with good dispositions, and as you value this inestimable treasure, to take measures for having them brought up betimes in his fear, and preserved from the corruption's and pollution's by which we have been surrounded.*[3]

CHAPTER 16

HOW PARENTS RESPOND TO PRODIGALS

The Father with Open Arms Receives the Son Who Had Gone Away

The pain and confusion that prodigal children bring has always torn the hearts out of parents and caused sleepless nights, nervous days, and tearful moments. As Calvin sought to bring the wisdom of Scripture to this reality, he seemed to be thrown on the merciful heart of the heavenly parent as a pattern for parents in pain. This is where Calvin placed the bulk of his counsel, for he had a mentor in the "Father of all mercies, and God of all comfort." He was an advocate of "the exuberance of parental kindness" and the "admirable example of mildness in a man." He notes that there are those who might "murmur at his compassion."

He acknowledges the sad situation of a son who is brought up with all the blessings of a good kingdom and yet is "moved by a blind and mad ambition" and being "destitute of sound judgment" to throw off parental love. He called this kind of behavior, "wicked arrogance," "ingratitude" and "foolish and insolent youth." But even when all seems to be lost, it is the kindness of God, that in the case of the prodigal son, "hunger proved to be the best teacher."

Emphasizing the tenderness of a father he summarizes the happy result as the "father not only pardons our sins in such a manner as to bury the remembrance of them, but even restores those gifts of which we had been deprived."

CALVIN SPEAKS:

The Exuberance of Paternal Kindness

Nor let us allege that we are justly rendered timid by a consciousness of sin, by which our Father, though mild and merciful, is daily offended. For if among men a son cannot have a better advocate to plead his cause with his father, and cannot employ a better intercessor to regain his lost favour, than if he come himself suppliant and downcast, acknowledging his fault, to implore the mercy of his father, whose paternal feelings cannot but be moved by such entreaties, what will that "Father of all mercies, and God of all comfort," do? (2 Cor. 1:3). Will he not rather listen to the tears and groans of his children, when supplicating for themselves (especially seeing he invites and exhorts us to do so), than to any advocacy of others to whom the timid have recourse, not without some semblance of despair, because they are distrustful of their father's mildness and clemency? The exuberance of his paternal kindness he sets before us in the parable (Luke 15:20) when the father with open arms receives the son who had gone away from him, wasted his substance in riotous living, and in all ways grievously sinned against him. He waits not till pardon is asked in words, but, anticipating the request, recognizes him afar off, runs to meet him, consoles him, and restores him to favour. By setting before us this admirable example of mildness in a man, he designed to show in how much greater abundance we may expect it from him who is not only a Father, but the best and most merciful of all fathers, however ungrateful, rebellious, and wicked sons we may be, provided only we throw ourselves upon his mercy. And the better to assure us that he is such a Father if we are Christians, he has been pleased to be called not only a Father, but our Father, as if we were pleading with him after this manner, O Father, who art possessed of so much affection for thy children, and art so ready to forgive, we thy children approach thee and present our requests, fully persuaded that thou hast no other feelings towards us than those of a father, though we are unworthy of such a parent. But as our narrow hearts are incapable of comprehending such boundless favour, Christ is not only the earnest and pledge of our adoption, but also gives us the Spirit as a witness of this adoption, that through him we may freely cry aloud, Abba, Father. Whenever, therefore, we are restrained by any feeling of hesitation, let us remember to ask of him that he may correct our timidity, and placing us under the magnanimous guidance of the Spirit, enable us to pray boldly.[1]

The Compassion of a Father

This parable is nothing else than a confirmation of the preceding doctrine. In the first part is shown how readily God is disposed to pardon our sins, and in the second part (which we shall afterwards treat in the proper place) is shown the great malignity and obstinacy of those who murmur at his compassion. In the person of a young prodigal who, after having been reduced to the deepest poverty by luxury and extravagance, returns as a suppliant to his father, to whom he had been disobedient and rebellious, Christ describes all sinners who, wearied of their folly, apply to the grace of God. To the kind father, on the other hand, who not only pardons the crimes of his son, but of his own accord meets him when returning, he compares God, who is not satisfied with pardoning those who pray to him, but even advances to meet them with the compassion of a father. Let us now examine the parable in detail.

And the younger of them said to his father. The parable opens by describing a mark of wicked arrogance in the youth, which appears in his being desirous to leave his father, and in thinking that he cannot be right without being permitted to indulge in debauchery, free from his father's control. There is also ingratitude in leaving the old man, and not only withholding the performance of the duties which be owed to him, but crippling and diminishing the wealth of his house. This is at length followed by wasteful luxury and wicked extravagance, by which he squanders all that he had. After so many offenses he deserved to find his father implacable.

Under this image our Lord unquestionably depicts to us the boundless goodness and inestimable forbearance of God, that no crimes, however aggravated, may deter us from the hope of obtaining pardon, There would be some foundation for the analogy, if we were to say that this foolish and insolent youth resembles those persons who, enjoying at the hand of God a great abundance of good things, are moved by a blind and mad ambition to be separated from Him, that they may enjoy perfect freedom; as if it were not more desirable than all the kingdoms of the world to live under the fatherly care and government of God. But as I am afraid that this allusion may be *thought overstrained, I shall satisfy myself with the literal meaning; not that I disapprove of the opinion, that under this figure is reproved the madness of those who imagine that it will be advantageous for them to have something of their own, and to be rich apart from the heavenly Father; but that I now confine myself within the limits of a Commentator.*

Christ here describes what usually happens with young men, when they are carried away by their natural disposition. Destitute of sound judgment, and maddened by passion, they are ill fitted for governing themselves, and are not restrained by fear or shame. It is therefore impossible but that they shall abandon themselves to every thing to which their sinful inclination prompts them, and rush on in a disgraceful course, till they are involved in shameful poverty. He afterwards describes the punishment which, in the righteous judgment of God, generally overtakes spendthrifts and prodigals. After having wickedly squandered their means, they are left to pine in hunger, and not having known how to use in moderation an abundant supply of the best bread, they are reduced to eat acorns and husks. In short, they become the companions of swine, and are made to feel that they are unworthy to partake of human food; for it is swinish gluttony to squander wickedly what was given for the support of life. As to the ingenious exposition which some have brought forward, that it is the just punishment of wicked scorn, when those who have rejected delicious bread in the house of our heavenly Father are driven by hunger to eat husks, it is a true and useful doctrine; but in the meantime, we must bear in mind the difference that exists between allegories and the natural meaning.

And was desirous to fill his belly. This means that, in consequence of hunger, he no longer thought of his former luxuries, but greedily devoured husks; for of that kind of food he could not be in want, when he was giving it to the swine. There is a well-known saying of Cyrus who, having for a long time suffered hunger during a flight, and having been slightly refreshed by eating coarse black bread, declared that he had never tasted savory bread till now; so the young man who is here mentioned was compelled by necessity to betake himself with appetite to husks. The reason is added, because no man gave to him; for the copulative conjunction and (kai) must, in my opinion, signify because, and what is here said does not refer to husks, which he had at hand, but I understand the meaning to be, that no man pitied his poverty; for prodigals who throw away the whole of their property are persons whom no man thinks himself bound to relieve, - nay more, as they have been accustomed to squander every thing, men think that nothing ought to be given to them.

And when he came to himself. Here is described to us the way in which God invites men to repentance. If of *their own accord they were wise, and became submissive, he would draw them more gently; but as they never stoop to obedience, till they have been subdued by the rod, he chastises them severely. Accordingly, to this young man, whom abundance rendered fierce and rebellious, hunger proved to be the best teacher. Instructed by this example, let us not imagine that God deals cruelly with us, if at any time he visits us with heavy afflictions; for in this manner those who were obstinate and intoxicated with mirth are taught by him to be obedient. In short, all the miseries which we endure are a profitable invitation to repentance. But as we are slow, we scarcely ever regain a sound mind, unless when we are forced by extreme distress; for until we are pressed by difficulties on every hand, and shut up to despair, the flesh always indulges in gaiety, or at least recoils. Hence we infer, that there is no reason to wonder, if the Lord often uses violent and even repeated strokes, in order to subdue our obstinacy, and, as the proverb runs, applies hard wedges to hard knots. It must also be observed, that the hope of bettering his condition, if he returned to his father, gave this young man courage to repent; for no severity of punishment will soften our depravity, or make us displeased with our sins, till we perceive some advantage. As this young man, therefore, is induced by confidence in his father's kindness to seek reconciliation, so the beginning of our repentance must be an acknowledgment of the mercy of God to excite in us favorable hopes.*

And while he was still afar off. This is the main point of the parable. If men, who are by nature prone to revenge, and too tenacious of their own rights, are moved by fatherly love kindly to forgive their children, and freely to bring them back, when they are sunk in wretchedness, God, whose boundless goodness exceeds all the affection of parents, will not treat us more harshly. And certainly nothing is here attributed to an earthly father which God does not promise with respect to himself. *Before they call, says he, I will answer* (Isaiah 65:24). That passage too of David is well known,

I said, I will acknowledge against me my unrighteousness to the Lord and thou forgavest the iniquity of my sin. (Psalm 32:5)

As this father, therefore, is not merely pacified by the entreaties of his son, but meets him when he is coming, and before he has heard a word, embraces him, filthy and ugly as he is, so God does not wait for a long prayer, but of his own free will meets the sinner as soon as he proposes to confess his fault.

It is wretched sophistry to infer from this, that the grace of God is not exhibited to sinners until they anticipate it by their repentance. "Here," say they, "is held out to us a father ready to pardon, but it is after that his son has begun to return to him; and therefore God does not look, and does not bestow his grace, on any but those who begin to seek him." It is, no doubt, true that, in order to his obtaining pardon, the sinner is required to have grief of conscience, and to be dissatisfied with himself; but it is wrong to infer from this, that repentance, which is the gift of God, is yielded by men from their own movement of their heart. And in this respect it would be improper to compare a mortal man to God; for it is not in the power of an earthly father to renew the stubborn heart of his son, as God changes hearts of stone into hearts of flesh. In short, the question here is not whether a man is converted by himself, and returns to him; but only under the figure of a man is commended the fatherly gentleness of God, and his readiness to grant forgiveness.

Father, I have sinned against heaven. Here is pointed out another branch of repentance, namely, such a conviction of sin as is accompanied by grief and shame. For he who is not grieved for having sinned, and whose offense is not placed before his eyes, will sooner attempt any thing than think of returning to the path of duty. Displeasure with sin must therefore go before repentance. And there is great emphasis in this expression, that the young man is said to have come to himself, as one whom the wanderings of wild desires had hurried away into forgetfulness of himself. And certainly so far astray are the impulses of the flesh, that any one who gives himself up to them may be said to have gone out of himself, and to have lost his senses. For this reason transgressors are commanded to return to the heart, (Isaiah 46:8.) Next follows a confession, not *such a one as the Pope has contrived, but one by which the son appeases his offended father; for this humility is absolutely necessary in order to obtain forgiveness of sins. This mode of expression, I have sinned against heaven, and before thee, is of the same import as if he had said, that God was offended in the person of an earthly father. And certainly this is the dictate of nature, that every one who rebels against a father rises wickedly also against God, who has placed children in subjection to parents.*

Bring out the best robe. Although in parables (as we have frequently observed) it would be idle to follow out every minute circumstance, yet it will be no violence to the literal meaning, if we say, that our heavenly Father not only pardons our sins in such a manner as to bury the remembrance of them, but even restores those gifts of which we had been deprived; as, on the other hand, by taking them from us, he chastises our ingratitude in order to make us feel ashamed at the reproach and disgrace of our nakedness.[2]

CHAPTER 17

HONOR AND OBEDIENCE TOWARD PARENTS

No one can despise his father without being guilty of an offense against God

C alvin knew that dishonor in the heart of a child or disobedience in behavior would mean that earthly blessings would be cut off from them. He taught that in the family, the "name of Father is...sacred" and no one can "despise his father without being guilty of an offense against God." He warned children of the dangers of disobedience declaring that "an inevitable curse threatens all stubborn and disobedient children." He noted how rare it is to find obedient children who honor their parents, asking, "for do we find one among a thousand that is obedient to his parents?" While parents are prone to exasperate their children and sin against them if they handle discipline in an ungodly manner, Calvin did not believe that this freed children from obedience to their parents. He declared that "[t]hose who abusively or stubbornly violate parental authority are monsters, not men!"

CALVIN SPEAKS:

Despising a Father Is Despising God

Honour thy father and thy mother: that thy days may be long upon the land which the LORD thy God giveth thee. - Exodus 20:12

It will be now well to ascertain what is the force of the word "honor," not as to its grammatical meaning, (for cabad, is nothing else but to pay due honor to God, and to men who are in authority), but as to its essential signification. Surely, since God would not have His servants comply with external ceremonies only, it cannot be doubted but that all the duties of piety towards parents are here comprised, to which children are laid under obligation by natural reason itself; and these may be reduced to three heads, i.e., that they should regard them with reverence; that they should obediently comply with their commands, and allow themselves to be governed by them, and that they should endeavor to repay what they owe to them, and thus heartily devote to them themselves and their services. Since, therefore, the name of Father is a sacred one, and is transferred to men by the peculiar goodness of God, the dishonoring of parents redounds to the dishonor of God Himself, nor can anyone despise his father without being guilty of an offense against God (sacrilegium). If any should object that there are many ungodly and wicked fathers whom their children cannot regard with honor without destroying the distinction between good and evil, the reply is easy, that the perpetual law of nature is not subverted by the sins of men; and therefore, however unworthy of honor a father may be, that he still retains, inasmuch as he is a father, his right over his children, provided it does not in anywise derogate from the judgment of God; for it is too absurd to think of absolving under any pretext the sins which are condemned by His Law; nay, it would be a base profanation to misuse the name of father for the covering of sins. In condemning, therefore, the vices of a father, a truly pious son will subscribe to God's Law; and still, whatsoever he may be, will acknowledge that he is to be honored, as being the father given him by God.

The third head of honor is, that children should take care of their parents, and be ready and diligent in all their duties towards them. This kind of piety the Greeks call ἀντιπελαργία, because storks supply food to their parents when they are feeble and worn out with old age, and are thus our instructors in gratitude. Hence the barbarity of those is all the more base and detestable, who either grudge or neglect to relieve the poverty of their parents, and to aid their necessities.[1]

Obedience of Children Enforced By the Authority of God

Children, obey your parents in the Lord: for this is right. Honour thy father and mother; (which is the first commandment with promise) That it may be well with thee, and thou mayest live long on the earth. And, ye fathers, provoke not your children to wrath: but bring them up in the nurture and admonition of the Lord. - Ephesians 6:1-4

Children, obey. Why does the apostle use the word obey instead of honor, which has a greater extent of meaning? It is because Obedience is the evidence of that honor which children owe to their parents, and is therefore more earnestly enforced. It is likewise more difficult; for the human mind recoils from the idea of subjection, and with difficulty allows itself to be placed under the control of another. Experience shews how rare this virtue is, for do we find one among a thousand that is obedient to his parents? By a figure of speech, a part is here put for the whole, but it is the most important part, and is necessarily accompanied by all the others.

In the Lord. Besides the law of nature, which is acknowledged by all nations, the obedience of children is enforced by the authority of God. Hence it follows, that parents are to be obeyed, so far only as is consistent with piety to God, which comes first in order. If the command of God is the rule by which the submission of children is to be regulated, it would be foolish to suppose that the performance of this duty could lead away from God himself.

For this is right. This is added in order to restrain the fierceness which, we have already said, appears to be natural to almost all men. He proves it to be right, because God has commanded it; for we are not at liberty to dispute, or call in question, the appointment of him whose will is the unerring rule of goodness and righteousness. That honor should be represented as including obedience is not surprising; for mere ceremony is of no value in the sight of God. The precept, honor thy father and mother, comprehends all the duties by which the sincere affection and respect of children to their parents can be expressed.

Which is the first commandment with promise. The promises annexed to the commandments are intended to excite our hopes, and to impart a greater cheerfulness to our obedience; and therefore Paul uses this as a kind of seasoning to render the submission, which he enjoins on children, more pleasant and agreeable. He does not merely say, that God has offered a reward to him who obeys his father and mother, but that such an offer is peculiar to this commandment. If each of the commandments had its own promises, there would have been no ground for the commendation bestowed in the present instance. But this is the first commandment, Paul tells us, which God has been pleased, as it were, to seal by a remarkable promise. There is some difficulty here; for the second commandment likewise contains a promise, "I am the Lord thy God, who shew mercy unto thousands of them that love me, and keep my commandments." (Exodus 20:5, 6) But this is universal, applying indiscriminately to the whole law, and cannot be said to be annexed to that commandment. Paul's assertion still holds true, that no other commandment but that which enjoins the obedience due by children to their parents is distinguished by a promise.[2]

Submission - a Step In Our Ascent To the Supreme Parent

But as this command to submit is very repugnant to the perversity of the human mind (which, puffed up with ambitious longings will scarcely allow itself to be subject), that superiority which is most attractive and least invidious is set forth as an example calculated to soften and bend our minds to habits of submission. From that subjection which is most easily endured, the Lord gradually accustoms us to every kind of legitimate subjection, the same principle regulating all. For to those whom he raises to eminences he communicates his authority, in so far as necessary to maintain their station. The titles of Father, God, and Lord, all meet in him alone and hence whenever any one of them is mentioned, our mind should be impressed with the same feeling of reverence. Those, therefore, to whom he imparts such titles, he distinguishes by some small spark of his refulgence, so as to entitle them to honour, each in his own place. In this way, we must consider that our earthly father possesses something of a divine nature in him, because there is some reason for his bearing a divine title, and that he who is our prince and ruler is admitted to some communion of honour with God.

And it makes no difference whether those on whom the honour is conferred are deserving or not. Be they what they may, the Almighty, by conferring their station upon them, shows that he would have them honoured. The commandment specifies the reverence due to those to whom we owe our being. This Nature herself should in some measure teach us. For they are monsters, and not men, who petulantly and contumeliously violate the paternal authority. Hence, the Lord orders all who rebel against their parents to be put to death, they being, as it where, unworthy of the light in paying no deference to those to whom they are indebted for beholding it. And it is evident, from the various appendices to the Law, that we were correct in stating, that the honour here referred to consists of three parts, reverence, obedience, and gratitude. The first of these the Lord enforces, when he commands that who curseth his father or his mother shall be put to death. In this way he avenges insult and contempt. The second he enforces, when he denounces the punishment of death on disobedient and rebellious children. To the third belongs our Saviour's declaration, that God requires us to do good to our parents (Matt. 15). And whenever Paul mentions this commandment, he interprets it as enjoining obedience.

A promise is added by way of recommendation, the better to remind us how pleasing to God is the submission which is here required. Paul applies that stimulus to rouse us from our lethargy, when he calls this the first commandment with promise; the promise contained in the First Table not being specially appropriated to any one commandment, but extended to the whole law. Whence this promise has, in like manner, reference to us also, inasmuch as the duration of the present life is a proof of the divine benevolence toward us. Wherefore, if any one who is obedient to parents happens to be cut off before mature age (a thing which not infrequently happens), the Lord nevertheless adheres to his promise as steadily as when he bestows a hundred acres of land where he had promised only one. The whole lies in this: We must consider that long life is promised only in so far as it is a blessing from God, and that it is a blessing only in so far as it is a manifestation of divine favour. This, however, he testifies and truly manifests to his servants more richly and substantially by death.

Therefore the submission yielded to them should be a step in our ascent to the Supreme Parent, and hence, if they instigate us to transgress the law, they deserve not to be regarded as parents, but as strangers attempting to seduce us from obedience to our true Father. The same holds in the case of rulers, masters, and superiors of every description. For it were unbecoming and absurd that the honour of God should be impaired by their exaltation - an exaltation which, being derived from him, ought to lead us up to him.[3]

Children to Be Obedient in All Things - What Does "All" Mean?

Children, obey your parents in all things:
for this is well pleasing unto the Lord. - Colossians 3:20

He enjoins it upon children to obey their parents, without any exception. But what if parents should feel disposed to constrain them to anything that is unlawful; will they in that case, too, obey without any reservation? Now it were worse than unreasonable, that the, authority of men should prevail at the expense of neglecting God. I answer, that here, too, we must understand as implied what he expresses elsewhere, (Ephesians 6:1) - in the Lord. But for what purpose does he employ a term of universality? I answer again, that it is to shew, that obedience must be rendered not merely to just commands, but also to such as are unreasonable. For many make themselves compliant with the wishes of their parents only where the command is not grievous or inconvenient. But, on the other hand, this one thing ought to be considered by children - that whoever may be their parents, they have been allotted to them by the providence of God, who by his appointment makes children subject to their parents.

In all things, therefore, that they may not refuse anything, however difficult or disagreeable - in all things, that in things indifferent they may give deference to the station which their parents occupy - in all things, that they may not put themselves on a footing of equality with their parents, in the way of questioning and debating, or disputing, it being always understood that conscience is not to be infringed upon. He prohibits parents from exercising an immoderate harshness, lest their children should be so disheartened as to be incapable of receiving any honorable training; for we see, from daily experience, the advantage of a liberal education.[4]

Long Life - A Gift of God in This Present Life

Children, obey your parents in the Lord: for this is right. Honour thy father and mother; (which is the first commandment with promise;) That it may be well with thee, and thou mayest live long on the earth. And, ye fathers, provoke not your children to wrath: but bring them up in the nurture and admonition of the Lord. - Ephesians 6:1-4

That it may be well with thee. The promise is a long life; from which we are led to understand that the present life is not to be overlooked among the gifts of God...Those who shew kindness to their parents from whom they derived life, are assured by God, that in this life it will be well with them.[5]

Forbidden: Detracting From the Dignity of Father and Mother

The purpose is: since the maintenance of his economy pleases the Lord God, the degrees of pre-eminence established by him ought to be inviolable for us. This, then, is the sum: that we should look up to those whom God has placed over us, and should treat them with honor, obedience, and gratefulness. It follows from this that we are forbidden to detract from their dignity either by contempt, by stubbornness, or by ungratefulness.[6]

Those Who Violate Parental Authority Are Monsters

For this reason, we ought not to doubt that the Lord has here established a universal rule. That is, knowing that someone has been placed over us by the Lord's ordination, we should render to him reverence, obedience, and gratefulness, and should perform such other duties for him as we can. It makes no difference whether our superiors are worthy or unworthy of this honor, for whatever they are they have attained their position through God's providence - a proof that the Lawgiver himself would have us hold them in honor. However, he has expressly bidden us to reverence our parents, who have brought us into this life. Nature itself ought in a way to teach us this. Those who abusively or stubbornly violate parental authority are monsters, not men! Hence the Lord commands that all those disobedient to their parents be put to death. For since they do not recognize those whose efforts brought them into the light of day, they are not worthy of its benefits. What we have noted is clearly true from various additions to the law, that there are three parts of the honor here spoken of: reverence, obedience, and gratefulness. The Lord confirms the first - reverence - when he enjoins that one who curses his father or mother be killed (Exodus 21:17; Leviticus 20:9; Proverbs 20:20); there he punishes contempt and abuse. He confirms the second - obedience - when he decrees the penalty of death for disobedient and rebellious children (Deuteronomy 21:18-21). What Christ says in Matthew chapter 5, refers to the third kind of honor, gratefulness; it is of God's commandment that we do good to our parents (verses 4-6). And whenever Paul mentions this commandment, he interprets it as requiring obedience (Ephesians 6:1-3; Colossians 3:20).[7]

Curses for Disobedient Children

Besides, while the Lord promises the blessing of the present life to those children who duly honor their parents, at the same time he implies that an inevitable curse threatens all stubborn and disobedient children. To assure that this commandment be carried out, he has, through his law, declared them subject to the sentence of death, and commanded that they undergo punishment. If they elude that judgment, he himself takes vengeance upon them in some way or other. For we see how many men of this sort perish either in battles or in quarrels; others are cast down in ways less common. Nearly all offer proof that this threatening is not in vain. Some people may escape punishment until extreme old age. Yet in this life they are bereft of God's blessing, and can only miserably pine away, being reserved for greater punishments to come. Far indeed, then, are they from sharing in the blessing promised to godly children! But we also ought in passing to note that we are bidden to obey our parents only "in the Lord".[8]

Punishment for Striking Father and Mother

For every one that curseth his father or his mother shall be surely put to death: he hath cursed his father or his mother; his blood shall be upon him. - Leviticus 20:9

The commandment is now sanctioned by the denunciation of capital punishment for its violation, yet not so as to comprehend all who have in any respect sinned against their parents, but sufficient to show that the rights of parents are sacred, and not to be violated without the greatest criminality. We know that parricides, [those who kill parents or close relatives] as being the most detestable of all men, were formerly sewn up in a leathern sack and cast into the water;* but God proceeds further, when He commands all those to be exterminated who have laid violent hands on their parents...or addressed them in abusive language. For to smite does not only mean to kill, but refers to any violence, although no wound may have been inflicted. If, then, any one had struck his father or mother with his fist, or with a stick, the punishment of such an act of madness was the same as for murder. And, assuredly, it is an abominable and monstrous thing for a son not to hesitate to assault those from whom he has received his life, nor can it be but that impunity

---

* *"By Roman Law parricides were sewn up in a leathern sack with a dog, a cock, a viper, and a monkey, and cast into the sea, or the nearest river."* -Vide Cicero pro Rosc. Amer.,ii.25,26 From p13 *Harmony of the Law* *accorded to so foul a crime must straightway produce cruel barbarism. The second law avenges not only violence done to parents, but also, abusive words, which soon proceed to grosser insults and atrocious contempt. Still, if any one should have lightly let drop some slight reproach, as is often the case in a quarrel, this severe punishment was not to be inflicted upon such, all inconsiderate piece of impertinence: and the word, kalal, from which the participle used by Moses is derived, not only means to reproach, but also to curse, as well as to esteem lightly, and to despise. Whilst, therefore, not every insult, whereby the reverence due to parents was violated, received the punishment of death, still God would have that impious pride, which would subvert the first principles of nature, held in abhorrence. But, inasmuch as it might seem hard that a word, however unworthy of a dutiful son, should be the cause of death, this objection is met, by what is added by God in Leviticus, "his blood shall be upon him, because he hath cursed his father or mother" as if He would put a stop to what men might otherwise presume to allege in mitigation of the severity of the punishment.*[9]

How to Respond To Parents Who Are Too Harsh

Should husbands and parents neglect their duty; should the latter be harsh and severe to the children whom they are enjoined not to provoke to anger, and by their severity harass them beyond measure; should the former treat with the greatest contumely the wives whom they are enjoined to love and to spare as the weaker vessels; would children be less bound in duty to their parents, and wives to their husbands? They are made subject to the froward and undutiful. Nay, since the duty of all is not to look behind them, that is, not to inquire into the duties of one another, but to submit each to his own duty, this ought especially to be exemplified in the case of those who are placed under the power of others. Wherefore, if we are cruelly tormented by a savage, if we are rapaciously pillaged by an avaricious or luxurious, if we are neglected by a sluggish, if, in short, we are persecuted for righteousness' sake by an impious and sacrilegious prince, let us first call up the remembrance of our faults, which doubtless the Lord is chastising by such scourges. In this way humility will curb our impatience.[10]

CHAPTER 18

THE MARRIAGES OF CHILDREN

It Is Not Lawful for Children to Contract Marriage, Except with the Consent of Parents

Cultural norms either do good or evil to young people in preparing them to marry. Like our day, sixteenth century Europe was struggling under the weight of its unbiblical premarital practices. Since Calvin sought to bring all things in subjection to the Word of God, it was natural for him to apply Scripture to the premarital life. He concluded that marriage was extremely important and that there should be high priority placed on it while celibacy should be rejected. He chastised those who were "immoderately extolling celibacy" and who would convince people to despise marriage. He believed that marriage was a "remedy for avoiding fornication" and that it was "not good for a man to be without a wife." He corrected the popular notion that a daughter could be forced into marriage against her consent. He prohibited marriages with unbelievers because it was "contracting marriages with the wicked" and contrary to Scripture. Calvin embraced "the common duty" of parents to help children get married. His view of parental authority was the guiding principle for his views of the premarital season of life, maintaining that it was "not lawful for the children of a family to contract marriage, except with the consent of parents." He expounded on good and bad reasons to marry. For example, he taught that it is wrong to marry someone out of mere physical lust "for marriage is a thing too sacred to allow that men should be induced to it by the lust of the eyes." He strongly counseled against "decrepit" old men marrying young ladies. He spoke against the Roman Catholic practice of childhood marriages and maintained that "marriage is not legitimate except between those who have reached puberty." In his commentaries, he also maintained that "True and valid engagements cannot be dissolved."

CALVIN SPEAKS:

The Dangers and Advantages of Singleness

Now concerning the things whereof ye wrote unto me:
It is good for a man not to touch a woman. - I Corinthians 7:1

As he had spoken of fornication, he now appropriately proceeds to speak of marriage which is the remedy for avoiding fornication. Now it appears, that, notwithstanding the greatly scattered state of the Corinthian Church, they still retained some respect for Paul, inasmuch as they consulted him on doubtful points. What their questions had been is uncertain, except in so far as we may gather them from his reply. This, however, is perfectly well known, that immediately after the first rise of the Church, there crept into it, through Satan's artifice, a superstition of such a kind, that a large proportion of them, through a foolish admiration of celibacy, despised the sacred connection of marriage; nay more, many regarded it with abhorrence, as a profane thing. This contagion had perhaps spread itself among the Corinthians also; or at least there were idly-disposed spirits, who, by immoderately extolling celibacy, endeavored to alienate the minds of the pious from marriage. At the same time, as the Apostle treats of many other subjects, he intimates that he had been consulted on a variety of points. What is chiefly of importance is, that we listen to his doctrine as to each of them.

It is good for a man. The answer consists of two parts. In the first, he teaches that it were good for everyone to abstain from connection with a woman, provided it was in his power to do so. In the second, he subjoins a correction to this effect, that as many cannot do this, in consequence of the weakness of their flesh, these persons must not neglect the remedy which they have in their power, as appointed for them by the Lord. Now we must observe what he means by the word good, when he declares that it is good to abstain from marriage, that we may not conclude, on the other hand, that the marriage connection is therefore evil - a mistake which Jerome has fallen into, not so much from ignorance, in my opinion, as from the heat of controversy. For though that great man was endowed with distinguished excellences, he labored, at the same time, under one serious defect, that when disputing he allowed himself to be hurried away into great extravagancies, so that he did not keep within the bounds of truth. The inference then which he draws is this "It is good not to touch a woman: it is therefore wrong to do so." Paul, however, does not make use of the word good here in such a signification as to be opposed to what is evil or vicious, but simply points out what is expedient on account of there being so many troubles, vexations, and anxieties that are incident to married persons. Besides, we must always keep in view the limitation which he subjoins. Nothing farther, therefore, can be elicited from Paul's words than this - that it is indeed expedient and profitable for a man not to be bound to a wife, provided he can do otherwise. Let us explain this by a comparison. Should any one speak in this way: "It were good for a man not to eat, or to drink, or to sleep" - he would not thereby condemn eating, or drinking, or sleeping, as things that *were wrong - but as the time that is devoted to these things is just so much taken from the soul, his meaning would be, that we would be happier if we could be free from these hindrances, and devote ourselves wholly to meditation on heavenly things. Hence, as there are in married life many impediments which keep a man entangled, it were on that account good not to be connected in marriage.[1]*

Is It Best to Be Married or Single?

But here another question presents itself, for these words of Paul have some appearance of inconsistency with the words of the Lord, in Genesis 2:18, where he declares, that it is not good for a man to be without a wife. What the Lord there pronounces to be evil Paul here declares to be good. I answer, that in so far as a wife is a help to her husband, so as to make his life happy, that is in accordance with God's institution; for in the beginning God appointed it so, that the man without the woman was, as it were, but half a man, and felt himself destitute of special and necessary assistance, and the wife is, as it were, the completing of the man. Sin afterwards came in to corrupt that institution of God; for in place of so great a blessing there has been substituted a grievous punishment, so that marriage is the source and occasion of many miseries. Hence, whatever evil or inconvenience there is in marriage, that arises from the corruption of the divine institution. Now, although there are in the meantime some remains still existing of the original blessing, so that a single life is often much more unhappy than the married life; yet, as married persons are involved in many inconveniences, it is with good reason that Paul teaches that it would be good for a man to abstain. In this way, there is no concealment of the troubles that are attendant upon marriage; and yet, in the meantime, there is no countenance given to those profane jests which are commonly in vogue with a view to bring it into discredit, such as the following: that a wife is a necessary evil, and that a wife is one of the greatest evils. For such sayings as these have come from Satan's workshop, and have a direct tendency to brand with disgrace God's holy institution.[2]

The Common Duty of Parents

And Abraham said unto his eldest servant of his house, that ruled over all that he had, Put, I pray thee, thy hand under my thigh. - Genesis 24:2

Abraham here fulfils the common duty of parents, in laboring for and being solicitous about the choice of a wife for his son: but he looks somewhat further; for since God had separated him from the Canaanites by a sacred covenant, he justly fears lest Isaac, by joining himself in affinity with them, should shake off the yoke of God. Some suppose that the depraved morals of those nations were so displeasing to him, that he conceived the marriage of his son must prove unhappy if he should take a wife from among them. But the special reason was, as I have stated, that he would not allow his own race to be mingled with that of the Canaanites, whom he knew to be already divinely appointed to destruction; yea, since upon their overthrow he was to be put into possession of the land, he was commanded to treat them with distrust as perpetual enemies. And although he had dwelt in tranquility among them for a time, yet he could not have a community of offspring with them without confounding things which, by the command of God, were to be kept distinct. Hence he wished both himself and his family to maintain this separation entire.[3]

Unequally Yoked

Be ye not unequally yoked together with unbelievers: for what fellowship hath righteousness with unrighteousness? And what communion hath light with darkness? - II Corinthians 6:14

Many are of opinion that he speaks of marriage, but the context clearly shows that they are mistaken. The word that Paul makes use of means - to be connected together in drawing the same yoke. It is a metaphor taken from oxen or horses, which require to walk at the same pace, and to act together in the same work, when fastened under one yoke. When, therefore, he prohibits us from having partnership with unbelievers in drawing the same yoke, he means simply this, that we should have no fellowship with them in their pollutions. For one sun shines upon us, we eat of the same bread, we breathe the same air, and we cannot altogether refrain from intercourse with them; but Paul speaks of the yoke of impiety, that is, of participation in works, in which Christians cannot lawfully have fellowship. On this principle marriage will also be prohibited, inasmuch as it is a snare, by which both men and women are entangled into an agreement with impiety; but what I mean is simply this, that Paul's doctrine is of too general a nature to be restricted to marriage exclusively, for he is discoursing here as to the shunning of idolatry, on which account, also, we are prohibited from contracting marriages with the wicked.[4]

On Marrying Idolaters

As long as we live among unbelievers, we cannot escape those dealings with them which relate to the ordinary affairs of life; but if we approach nearer, so that a greater intimacy should arise, we open the door as it were to Satan. Such are alliances between kings and nations, and for the ancient people. And although our condition now-a-days is more free, still we are warned that all temptations are to be avoided which might give occasion to this evil. It is notorious that men are too apt to be led away by the blandishments of their wives; and also, that men in their power compel their wives to obedience. Those, therefore, who mix with idolaters, knowingly and willfully devote themselves to idols.[5]

They Have Polluted Holiness and Married Foreign Wives

Some take, kodash, for the sanctuary or the temple; others for the keeping of the law; but I prefer to apply it to the covenant itself; and we might suitably take it in a collective sense, except the simpler meaning be more approved - that Judah polluted his separation. As to the Prophet's object and the subject itself, he charges them here, I have no doubt, with profanation, because the Jews rendered themselves vile, though God had consecrated them to himself. They had then polluted holiness, even when they had been separated from the world; for they had disregarded so great an honor, by which they might have been pre-eminent, had they continued in their integrity. It may be also taken collectively, they have polluted holiness, that is, they have polluted that nation which has been separated from other nations: but as this exposition may seem hard and somewhat strained, I am inclined to think that what is here meant is that separation by which the Jews were known from other nations. But yet what I have stated may serve to remove whatever obscurity there may be. And that this holiness ought to be referred to that gratuitous election by which God had adopted the Jews as his peculiar people, is evident from what the Prophet says, that they married foreign wives. We then see the purpose of this passage, which is to show, that the Jews were

*ungrateful to God, because they mingled with heathen
nations, and knowingly and willfully cast aside that glory
by which God had adorned them by choosing them, as
Moses says, to be to him a royal priesthood (Exodus 19:6).
Holiness, we know, was much recommended to the Jews,
in order that they might not abandon themselves to any of
the pollutions of the heathens. Hence God had forbidden
them under the law to take foreign wives, except they were
first purified, as we find in Deuteronomy 21:11, 12; if any
one wished to marry a captive, she was to have her head
shaven and her nails pared; by which it was intimated,
that such women were impure, and that their husbands
would be contaminated, except they were first purified.*[6]

Marrying for the Sake of Beauty

*And Jacob loved Rachel; and said, I will serve thee seven years for
Rachel thy younger daughter. - Genesis 29:18*

*Further, it is not altogether to be deemed a fault that Jacob
was rather inclined to love Rachel; whether it was that
Leah, on account of her tender eyes, was less beautiful, or
that she was pleasing only by the comeliness of her eyes,
while Rachel excelled her altogether in elegance of form.
For we see how naturally a secret kind of affection produces
mutual love. Only excess is to be guarded against, and
so much the more diligently, because it is difficult so to
restrain affections of this kind, that they do not prevail to*

the stifling of reason. Therefore he who shall be induced to choose a wife, because of the elegance of her form, will not necessarily sin, provided reason always maintains the ascendancy, and holds the wantonness of passion in subjection. Yet perhaps Jacob sinned in being too self-indulgent, when he desired Rachel the younger sister to be given to him, to the injury of the elder; and also, while yielding to the desire of his own eyes, he undervalued the virtues of Leah: for this is a very culpable want of self government, when any one chooses a wife only for the sake of her beauty, whereas excellence of disposition ought to be deemed of the first importance. But the strength and ardor of his attachment manifests itself in this, that he felt no weariness in the labor of seven years: but chastity was also joined with it, so that he persevered, during this long period, with a patient and quiet mind in the midst of so many labors. And here again the integrity and continence of that age is apparent, because, though dwelling under the same roof, and accustomed to familiar intercourse, Jacob yet conducted himself with modesty, and abstained from all impropriety. Therefore, at the close of the appointed time he said, "Give me my wife, that I may go in unto her," by which he implies that she had been hitherto a pure virgin.[7]

Choosing a Wife for the Elegance of Her Form

And Jacob loved Rachel; and said, I will serve thee seven years for
Rachel thy younger daughter. - Genesis 29:18

Therefore he who shall be induced to choose a wife, because of the elegance of her form, will not necessarily sin, provided reason always maintains the ascendancy, and holds the wantonness of passion in subjection. Yet perhaps Jacob sinned in being too self-indulgent, when he desired Rachel the younger sister to be given to him, to the injury of the elder; and also, while yielding to the desire of his own eyes, he undervalued the virtues of Leah: for this is a very culpable want of self government, when any one chooses a wife only for the sake of her beauty, whereas excellence of disposition ought to be deemed of the first importance.[8]

Marriage Is Too Sacred for the Lust of the Eyes

And it came to pass, when men began to multiply on the face of the earth, and daughters were born unto them, that the sons of God saw the daughters of men that they were fair; and they took them wives of all which they chose. And the LORD said, My spirit shall not always strive with man, for that he also is flesh: yet his days shall be an hundred and twenty years. There were giants in the earth in those days; and also after that, when the sons of God came in unto the daughters of men, and they bare children to them, the same became mighty men which were of old, men of renown. - Genesis 6:1-4

Moses does not deem it worthy of condemnation that regard was had to beauty, in the choice of wives; but that mere lust reigned. For marriage is a thing too sacred to allow that men should be induced to it by the lust of the eyes. For this union is inseparable comprising all the parts of life; as we have before seen, that the woman was created to be a helper of the man. Therefore our appetite becomes brutal, when we are so ravished with the charms of beauty, that those things which are chief are not taken into the account. Moses more clearly describes the violent impetuosity of their lust, when he says, that they took wives of all that they chose; by which he signifies, that the sons of God did not make their choice from those possessed of necessary endowments, but wandered without discrimination, rushing onward according to their lust. We are taught, however, in these words, that temperance is to be used in holy wedlock, and that its profanation is no light crime before God.[9]

Intermarrying in Families

None of you shall approach to any that is near of kin to him, to uncover their nakedness: I am the LORD. - Leviticus 18:6

None of you shall approach to any that is near. This name does not include all female relations; for cousin-germans of the father's or mother's side are permitted to intermarry; but it must be restricted to the degrees, which He proceeds *to enumerate, and is merely a brief preface, declaring that there are certain degrees of relationship which render marriages incestuous. We may, therefore, define these female relations of blood to be those which are spoken of immediately afterwards, viz., that a son should not marry his mother, nor a son-in-law his mother-in-law; nor a paternal or maternal uncle his niece, nor a grandfather his granddaughter, nor a brother his sister, nor a nephew his paternal or maternal aunt, or his uncle's wife, nor a father-in-law his daughter-in-law, nor a brother-in-law his brother's wife, nor a step-father his stepdaughter. The Roman laws accord with the rule prescribed by God, as if their authors had learnt from Moses what was decorous and agreeable to nature. The phrase which God uses frequently "to uncover the turpitude," is intended to awaken abhorrence, in order that the Israelites may beware more diligently of all incest. The Hebrew word, indeed, gnervah, signifies nakedness, therefore some translate it actively, "the nakedness of thy father," i e., the womb which thy father hath uncovered; but this meaning would not be suitable to the nakedness of thy daughter, or thy daughter-in-law, or thy sister. Consequently, there is no doubt but that Moses means to denote that it is a filthy and shameful thing.*[10]

Why Did He Refuse an Opportunity for Marriage?

Nevertheless, in the midst of such commotions as these, I am so much at my ease, as to have the audacity to think, of taking a wife. A certain damsel of noble rank has been proposed to me, and with a fortune above my condition. Two considerations deterred me from that connection - because she did not understand our language, and because I feared she might be too mindful of her family and education. Her brother, a very devout person, urged the connection, and on no other account than that, blinded by his affection to me, he neglected his own interests. His wife also, with a like partiality, contended, as he did, so that I would have been prevailed upon to submit with a good grace, unless the Lord had otherwise appointed. When, thereupon, I replied that I could not engage myself unless the maiden would undertake that she would apply her mind to the learning of our language, she requested time for deliberation. Thereupon, without further parley, I sent my brother, with a certain respectable man, to escort hither another, who, if she answers her repute, will bring a dowry large enough, without any money at all. Indeed, she is mightily commended by those who are acquainted with her. If it come to pass, as we may certainly hope will be the case, the marriage ceremony will not be delayed beyond the tenth of March.[11]

A Daughter's Willing Consent

And Caleb said, He that smiteth Kirjath-sepher, and taketh it, to him will I give Achsah my daughter to wife. And Othniel the son of Kenaz, the brother of Caleb, took it: and he gave him Achsah his daughter to wife. - Joshua 15:16-17

Although it is the office of parents to settle their daughters in life, they are not permitted to exercise tyrannical power and assign them to whatever husbands they think fit without consulting them. For while all contracts ought to be voluntary, freedom ought to prevail especially in marriage that no one may pledge his faith against his will. But Caleb was probably influenced by the belief that his daughter would willingly give her consent, as she could not modestly reject such honorable terms; for the husband to be given her was no common man, but one who should excel all others in warlike prowess. It is quite possible, however, that Caleb in the heat of battle inconsiderately promised what it was not in his power to perform. It seems to me, however, that according to common law, the agreement implied the daughter's consent, and was only to take effect if it was obtained. God certainly heard the prayer of Caleb, when he gave him a son-in-law exactly to his mind. For had the free choice been given him, there was none whom he would have preferred.[12]

Breaking Marriage Engagements

True and valid engagements cannot be dissolved any more than consummated marriages, since God's commands also apply here: "What God has joined together, let not man put asunder." They cannot be broken by mutual consent of both parties, far less by the will of either party as once was tolerated by the Romans, and even by Moses because of the stubbornness of the Jews.[13]

The Seriousness of Betrothal

If a damsel that is a virgin he betrothed unto an husband, and a man find her in the city, and lie with her. - Deuteronomy 22:23

The severity of the punishment is now extended further, and a betrothed woman is counted as a wife; and this for a very good reason, because she has plighted her troth, and it is a token of abandoned incontinency for the mind of a woman to be so alienated from the man to whom she is betrothed, as to prostitute her virginity to another's embraces. But since one who has been ravished is not criminal, a woman is absolved if she be forced in a field, because it is probable that she yielded unwillingly, inasmuch as she was far from assistance. Although, however, the terms are accommodated to the comprehension of a rude people, it was the intention of God to distinguish force from consent. Thus if a girl had been forced in a retired part of a building, from whence her cries could not be heard, God would undoubtedly have her acquitted, provided she could prove her innocence by satisfactory testimony and conjecture.[14]

"But if her father disallow her." *The expression is remarkable, "And the Lord shall forgive her," whereby Moses gently reproves the foolish thoughtlessness of the girl; and soon afterwards the same thing is spoken of married women. And surely their rashness is worthy of reprehension, if unmindful of their condition, they, as it were, shake off the yoke and hastily commit themselves. God therefore hints that they are not without blame; but lest they should be tormented by secret remorse, He removes every scruple, declaring that He will forgive, if the performance of the vow shall have been prevented in any other quarter. When the dissent of the father or the husband is required on the same day, it is tantamount to saying that what they have once approved of cannot be disallowed. Further, to "hold his peace" to a wife or daughter, signifies that he does not oppose, but give by silence a token of consent.*[15]

So far as respects marital fidelity, from the time that a young woman was engaged to a man, she was regarded by the Jews to be his lawful wife. When a "woman engaged to a husband" was convicted of being unchaste, the law condemned both the guilty parties as adulterers.[16]

Fathers Held Responsible for Proofs of Virginity

If any man take a wife, and go in unto her, and hate her. - Deuteronomy 22:13

This passage also tends to the exaltation of chastity. God provides against both cases, lest a husband should unjustly bring reproach upon a chaste and innocent young woman, and lest a young woman, having been defiled, should escape punishment, if she pretended to be a virgin. A third object is also to be remarked, viz., that parents were thus admonished to be more careful in watching over their children. This is, indeed, an act of gross brutality, that a husband, wittingly and willingly, should seek a false pretext for divorcing his wife by bringing reproach and infamy upon her; but, since it does not infrequently happen that the libidinous become disgusted with their vices, and then endeavor to rid themselves of them in every way, it was needful to correct this evil, and to prescribe a method whereby the integrity of the woman should be safe from the calumnies of an ungodly and cruel husband; whilst it was also just to give relief to an honest man, lest he should be compelled to cherish in his bosom a harlot, by whom he had been deceived; for it is a very bitter thing to ingenuous minds silently to endure so great an ignominy. An admirable precaution is here laid down, i.e., that if a woman were accused by her husband, it was in the power of her parents to produce the tokens of chastity which should acquit her; but if they did not, that the husband should not be obliged against his will to keep her in his house, after she had been defiled by another. It is plain from this passage, that the tokens of virginity were taken on a cloth, on the first night of marriage, as future proofs of chastity. It is also probable that the cloth was laid up before witnesses as a pledge, to be a sure defense for pure and modest young women; for it would have been giving too much scope to the parents if it had been believed simply on their evidence; but Moses speaks briefly as of a well-known custom.[17]

Children Getting Married

It has always been judged and rightfully so, that marriage is not legitimate except between those who have reached puberty. When a boy marries a girl, this is a childish game, and the sort of levity that deserved punishment.

First of all, it must be stated that those who are under the authority of their parents or guardians are not free or independent, especially in this matter. Even if the parents or guardians consent, or even if they are the principal instigators of the marriage-nonetheless, the contracts made before the proper age do not bind the children unless, after they reach puberty, they fell the same way, and voluntarily acknowledge that they consider their premature marriage valid.

If any parents betroth their children before they reach puberty, and pledge themselves and their possessions, they nevertheless cannot bind the children who are not yet ready for marriage. A contract of this sort is a profaning of marriage. If anyone has rashly put himself in a guilty position, let him bear the punishment he deserves. The terms of marriage cannot be carried out, since the children, when they reach puberty, are free to retract whatever their parents wrongfully contracted on their part. [18]

Children Who Commit to Marriage Without Parental Consent

And Abraham said unto his eldest servant of his house, that ruled over all that he had, Put, I pray thee, thy hand under my thigh: And I will make thee swear by the LORD, the God of heaven, and the God of the earth, that thou shalt not take a wife unto my son of the daughters of the Canaanites, among whom I dwell: But thou shalt go unto my country, and to my kindred, and take a wife unto my son Isaac. - Genesis 24:2-4

Now this example should be taken by us as a common rule, to show that it is not lawful for the children of a family to contract marriage, except with the consent of parents; and certainly natural equity dictates that, in a matter of such importance, children should depend upon the will of their parents. How detestable, therefore, is the barbarity of the Pope, who has dared to burst this sacred bond asunder! Wherefore the wantonness of youths is to be restrained, that they may not rashly contract nuptials without consulting their fathers. [19]

Old Men Marrying Younger Women

If a decrepit old man falls in love with a young girl, it is because of his base and shameful lust. He will defraud her if he marries her.[21]

A Coerced Vow to Marry Made Null

Dear Sir and Brothers: Insofar as you have found it desirable to request our counsel and advice concerning the marriage vows between M. Jean Focard and Margueritte Heberarde — that is, whether their vows are valid — we, having assembled in the name of God, are in accord to offer the following.

Having reviewed the acts and proceedings that we extracted from your registrar, concerning what Margueritte said, her mother and sister tell us, quite flatly, that the girl was deceived and that they forced her into it. Her aunt — the widow of M. Pierre Focard — as well as his brother-in-law and servant, have also sworn that they knew of this all along....[W]e note that although a ceremony for the exchanging of marriage vows occurred, not a single witness swears that the girl said anything by way of consent.... Furthermore, M. Jean Focard himself affirms that he has not had an opportunity to speak to Margueritte for some time and that he has never understood what she actually said at their wedding. Therefore, given the present facts, we cannot rule that a marriage occurred. Rather, since the act took place contrary to order and reason, we judge it to be null.

Nevertheless, since this is a delicate matter and could cause a great deal of conflict between the parties, and, in order to forestall any unfortunate repercussions as well as to prevent future rumors and reproach, we are of the opinion that M. Focard should summon the mother and the girl before the common court and there have the marriage annulled. The two should solemnly swear and confirm what they have attested to be true. In any event, in our definitive judgment, their marriage vows are null, and each party is free to marry someone else.[21]

THE FAMILY AT CHURCH

Reverence Should Always Be Shown To Older Persons

C alvin assumed that families would be together in the assembly, and in his expositions he spoke to family members of all ages and all walks of life.

Regarding intergenerational relationships in the church, he particularly felt it was appropriate for ministers to understand that "reverence should always be shewn to older persons." In all areas, Calvin believed that church members should be treated as family members.

The family life of an elder was a critical component in the relationship of church and family. In Calvin's scheme, the pastor's "whole family ought to be a sort of mirror of chaste and honorable discipline." Calvin made it clear that the "apostle does not recommend a clever man, and deeply skilled in domestic matters, but one who has learned to govern a family by wholesome discipline."

The guiding lights for Calvin regarding gender roles in the church were the commands of Scripture and the "creation order" roles and responsibilities. These two formed Calvin's view of gender distinctions. Like John Knox after him, he asserted that "the government of women" was "a monstrous thing." Contrary to the pattern of modern times, Calvin believed that women had a distinct and contrasting role compared to men in the church. They were not created for leadership or "public management of affairs" and were "prohibited from authority to teach in public." This prohibition was not the end of their ministries in the church, however, for he also urged older women to teach the younger women. Further, he held that this restriction was not a broad principle for all of life, but was only to be upheld in "a duly regulated assembly."

Calvin Speaks:

Relating With Spiritual Fathers - Don't Spare or Indulge

Rebuke not an elder, but entreat him as a father; and the younger men as brethren. - I Timothy 5:1

Do not harshly rebuke an elder. He now recommends to Timothy gentleness and moderation in correcting faults. Correction is a medicine, which has always some bitterness, and consequently is disagreeable. Besides, Timothy being a young man, his severity would have been less tolerable, if it had not been somewhat moderated.

But exhort him as a father. The Apostle enjoins him to reprove elder persons as parents; and he even employs the milder term, exhort. It is impossible not to be moved with reverence, when we place before our eyes our father or our mother; in consequence of which, instead of harsher vehemence, we are immediately influenced by modesty. Yet it ought to be observed, that he does not wish old men to be spared or indulged in such a manner as to sin with impunity and without correction; he only wishes that some respect should be paid to their age, that they may more patiently bear to be admonished.[1]

Gentleness with Brothers in the Church

Rebuke not an elder, but entreat him as a father; and the younger men as brethren. - I Timothy 5:1

The younger as brethren. Even towards younger persons he wishes moderation to be used, though not in an equal degree; for the vinegar must always be mingled with oil, but with this difference, that reverence should always be shewn to older persons, and equals should be treated with brotherly gentleness. Hence pastors are taught, that they must not only take into account their office, but must also see particularly what is due to the age of individuals; for the same things are not applicable to all. Let it therefore be remembered, that, if dramatic performers attend to decorum on the stage, it ought not to be neglected by pastors, who occupy so lofty a station.[2]

The Marriage of an Elder

If any be blameless, the husband of one wife, having faithful children not accused of riot or unruly. - Titus 1:6

The husband of one wife. The reason why this rule is laid down - has been explained by us in the Commentary on the First Epistle to Timothy. Polygamy was so common among the Jews, that the wicked custom had nearly passed into a law. If any man had married two wives before he made a profession of Christianity, it would have been cruel to compel him to divorce one of them; and therefore the apostles endured what was in itself faulty, because they could not correct it. Besides, they who had involved themselves by marrying more than one wife at a time, even though they had been prepared to testify their repentance by retaining but one wife, had, nevertheless, given a sign of their incontinence, which might have been a brand on their good name. (The meaning is the same as if Paul had enjoined them to elect those who had lived chastely in marriage - had been satisfied with having a single wife, and had forbidden those who had manifested the power of lust by marrying many wives. At the same time, he who, having become an unmarried man by the death of his wife, marries another, ought, nevertheless, to be accounted "the husband of one wife;" for the apostle does not say, that they shall choose him who has been, but him who is, "the husband of one wife."[3]

The Children of an Elder

If any be blameless, the husband of one wife, having faithful children not accused of riot or unruly. - Titus 1:6

Seeing that it is required that a pastor shall have prudence and gravity, it is proper that those qualities should be exhibited in his family; for how shall that man who cannot rule his own house - be able to govern the church! Besides, not only must the bishop himself be free from reproach, but his whole family ought to be a sort of mirror of chaste and honorable discipline; and, therefore, in the First Epistle to Timothy, he not less strictly enjoins their wives what they ought to be. First, he demands that the children shall be "believers;" whence it is obvious that they have been educated in the sound doctrine of godliness, and in the fear of the Lord. Secondly, that they shall not be devoted to luxury, that they may be known to have been educated to temperance and frugality. Thirdly, that they shall not be disobedient; for he who cannot obtain from his children any reverence or subjection will hardly be able to restrain the people by the bridle of discipline.[4]

Ruling a Family Trains and Adapts a Man for Ruling a Church

One that ruleth well his own house, having his children in subjection with all gravity. - I Timothy 3:4

Who ruleth well his own house. Hence it is evident, that Paul does not demand that a bishop shall be unacquainted within human life, but that he shall be a good and praiseworthy master of a household; for, whatever may be the admiration commonly entertained for celibacy and a philosophical life altogether removed from ordinary *custom, yet wise and thoughtful men are convinced by experience, that they who are not ignorant of ordinary life, but are practiced in the duties of human intercourse, are better trained and adapted for governing the Church. And, therefore, we ought to observe the reason which is added (1 Timothy 3:5), that he who does not know how to rule his family, will not be qualified for governing the Church. Now, this is the case with very many persons, and indeed with almost all who have been drawn out of an idle and solitary life, as out of dens and caverns, for they are a sort of savages and destitute of humanity.*

Who hath his children in subjection with, all reverence. The apostle does not recommend a clever man, and deeply skilled in domestic matters, but one who has learned to govern a family by wholesome discipline. He speaks chiefly of children, who may be expected to possess the natural disposition of their father, and therefore it will be a great disgrace to a bishop, if he has children who lead a wicked and scandalous life. As to wives, he will speak of them afterwards; but at present, as I have said, he glances at the most important part of a house.

In the Epistle to Titus, (Titus 1:6) he shows what is here meant by the word reverence; for, after having said that the children of a bishop must not be unruly and disobedient, he likewise adds, "nor liable to the reproach of profligacy or of intemperance." He therefore means, in a word, that their morals shall be regulated by all chastity, modesty, and gravity.[5]

Women Speaking in a
"Duly Regulated Assembly"

Let your women keep silence in the churches: for it is not permitted unto them to speak; but they are commanded to be under obedience, as also saith the law. And if they will learn anything, let them ask their husbands at home: for it is a shame for women to speak in the church. - I Corinthians 14:34-35

It appears that the Church of the Corinthians was infected with this fault too, that the talkativeness of women was allowed a place in the sacred assembly, or rather that the fullest liberty was given to it. Hence he forbids them to speak in public, either for the purpose of teaching or of prophesying. This, however, we must understand as referring to ordinary service, or where there is a Church in a regularly constituted state; for a necessity may occur of such a nature as to require that a woman should speak in public; but Paul has merely in view what is becoming in a duly regulated assembly.[6]

What Does the Law Have to
Do with Women Speaking in Church?

What connection has the object that he has in view with the subjection under which the law places women? "For what is there," someone will say, "to hinder their being in subjection, and yet at the same time teaching?" I answer, that the office of teaching is a superiority in the Church, and is, consequently, inconsistent with subjection. For how unseemly a thing it were, that one who is under subjection to one of the members, should preside over the entire body! It is therefore an argument from things inconsistent - If the woman is under subjection, she is, consequently, prohibited from authority to teach in public. And unquestionably, wherever even natural propriety has been maintained, women have in all ages been excluded from the public management of affairs. It is the dictate of common sense, that female government is improper and unseemly... Paul's reasoning, however, is simple - that authority to teach is not suitable to the station that a woman occupies, because, if she teaches, she presides over all the men, while it becomes her to be under subjection.

If they wish to learn anything. That he may not seem, by this means, to shut out women from opportunities of learning, he desires them, if they are in doubt as to anything, to inquire in private, that they may not stir up any disputation in public. When he says, husbands, he does not prohibit them from consulting the Prophets themselves, if necessary. For all husbands are not competent to give an answer in such a case; but, as he is reasoning here as to external polity, he reckons it sufficient to point out what is unseemly, that the Corinthians may guard against it.[7]

When Can Women Teach?

Let the woman learn in silence with all subjection. But I suffer not a woman to teach, nor to usurp authority over the man, but to be in silence. - I Timothy 2:11-12

Let a woman learn in quietness. After having spoken of dress, he now adds with what modesty women ought to conduct themselves in the holy assembly. And first he bids them learn quietly; for quietness means silence that they may not take upon them to speak in public. This he immediately explains more clearly, by forbidding them to teach.

But I suffer not a woman to teach. Not that he takes from them the charge of instructing their family, but only excludes them from the office of teaching, which God has committed to men only. On this subject we have explained our views in the exposition of the First Epistle to the Corinthians. If anyone bring forward, by way of objection, Deborah (Judges 4:4) and others of the same class, of whom we read that they were at one time appointed by the commend of God to govern the people, the answer is easy. Extraordinary acts done by God do not overturn the ordinary rules of government, by which he intended that we should be bound. Accordingly, if women at one time held the office of prophets and teachers, and that too when they were supernaturally called to it by the Spirit of God, He who is above all law might do this; but, being a peculiar case, this is not opposed to the constant and ordinary system of government. He adds - what is closely allied to the office of teaching - and not to assume authority over the man; for the very reason, why they are forbidden to teach, is, that it is not permitted by their condition. They are subject, and to teach implies the rank of power or authority. Yet it may be thought that there is no great force in this argument, because even prophets and teachers are subject to kings and to other magistrates. I reply, there is no absurdity in the same person commanding and likewise obeying, when viewed in different relations. But this does not apply to the case of woman, who by nature (that is, by the ordinary law of God) is formed to obey; for gunaikokrati (the government of women) has always been regarded by all wise persons as a monstrous thing, and, therefore, so to speak, it will be a mingling of heaven and earth, if women usurp the right to teach. Accordingly, he bids them be "quiet," that is, keep within their own rank.[8]

Older Women Keeping Younger Women from Imprudence

That they may teach the young women to be sober, to love their husbands, to love their children, to be discreet, chaste, keepers at home, good, obedient to their own husbands, that the word of God be not blasphemed. - Titus 2:4-5

That they may be more attentive to duty, he shows that it is not enough if their own life be decent, if they do not also train young women, by their instructions, to a decent and chaste life. He therefore adds, that by their example they should train to temperance and gravity those younger women whom the warmth of youth might otherwise lead into imprudence.

To love their husbands and their children. I do not agree with those who think that this is a recapitulation of the advices which elderly women should give to those who are younger for a careful perusal of the context will enable any one easily to perceive that Paul goes on in explaining the duties of women, which apply equally to those who are older. Besides, the construction would be inappropriate, σωφρονίζωσι, σώφρονας εἶναι. Yet while he instructs elderly females what they ought to be, he at the same time holds out to the younger the example which they ought to follow. Thus he indiscriminately teaches both. In short, he wishes women to be restrained, by conjugal love and affection for their children, from giving themselves up to licentious attachments, he wishes them to rule their own house in a sober and orderly manner, forbids them to wander about in public places, bids them be chaste, and at the same time modest, so as to be subject to the dominion of their husbands; for those who excel in other virtues sometimes take occasion from them to act haughtily, so as to be disobedient to their husbands.

When he adds, that the word of God may not be evil spoken of, it is supposed that this relates strictly to women who were married to unbelieving husbands, who might judge of the gospel from the wicked conduct of their wives; and this appears to be confirmed by 1 Peter 3:1. But what if he does not speak of husbands alone? And, indeed, it is probable that he demands such strictness of life as not to bring the gospel into the contempt of the public by their vices. As to the other parts of the verse, the reader will find them explained in the Commentary on the First Epistle to Timothy.[9]

CHAPTER 20

MODESTY

To Adorn Themselves Sparingly and Modestly Without Pomp and Ambition

As with all other areas of life, Calvin believed that women should be informed by Scripture instead of their own affections or social environments. Modest dress was a protection for women and a special adornment. Modesty was designed to "free the heart from inward cupidity," and it was "the ornament of the soul." While their primary adornment needed to be spiritual, he taught that they should guard against extremes and keep themselves from "sumptuous or costly adorning." At the same time, he asserted that it would be an "immoderate strictness wholly to forbid neatness and elegance in clothing." Modesty of the women in the gatherings of the church was a concern for Calvin. He wrote that in their apparel, they "seldom hit the golden mean."

CALVIN SPEAKS:

The Spiritual Adorning of the Soul

Whose adorning let it not be that outward adorning of plaiting the hair, and of wearing of gold, or of putting on of apparel; But let it be the hidden man of the heart, in that which is not corruptible, even the ornament of a meek and quiet spirit, which is in the sight of God of great price. - I Peter 3:3-4

Whose adorning. The other part of the exhortation is, that wives are to adorn themselves sparingly and modestly: for we know that they are in this respect much more curious and ambitious than they ought to be. Then Peter does not without cause seek to correct in them this vanity. And though he reproves generally sumptuous or costly adorning, yet he points out some things in particular, - that they were not artificially to curl or wreath their hair, as it was usually done by crisping-pins, or otherwise to form it according to the fashion; nor were they to set gold around their head: for these are the things in which excesses especially appear. It may be now asked, whether the Apostle wholly condemns the use of gold in adorning the body. Were any one to urge these words, it may be said, that he prohibits precious garments no less than gold;

for he immediately adds, the putting on of apparel, or, of clothes. But it would be an immoderate strictness wholly to forbid neatness and elegance in clothing. If the material is said to be too sumptuous, the Lord has created it; and we know that skill in art has proceeded from him. Then Peter did not intend to condemn every sort of ornament, but the evil of vanity, to which women are subject. Two things are to be regarded in clothing, usefulness and decency; and what decency requires is moderation and modesty. Were, then, a woman to go forth with her hair wantonly curled and decked, and make an extravagant display, her vanity could not be excused. They who object and say, that to clothe one's-self in this or that manner is an indifferent thing, in which all are free to do as they please, may be easily confuted; for excessive elegance and superfluous display, in short, all excesses, arise from a corrupted mind. Besides, ambition, pride, affectation of display, and all things of this kind, are not indifferent things. Therefore they whose minds are purified from all vanity, will duly order all things, so as not to exceed moderation.

But let it be the hidden, man of the heart. The contrast here ought to be carefully observed. Cato said, that they who are anxiously engaged in adorning the body, neglect the adorning of the mind; so Peter, in order to restrain this desire in women, introduces a remedy, that they are to devote themselves to the cultivation of their minds. The word heart, no doubt means the whole soul. He at the same time shews in what consists the spiritual adorning of women, even in the incorruptness of a meek and quiet spirit. "Incorruptness," as I think, is set in opposition to things which fade and vanish away, things which serve to adorn the body. Therefore the version of Erasmus departs from the real meaning. In short, Peter means that the ornament of the soul is not like a fading flower, nor consists in vanishing splendor, but is incorruptible. By mentioning quiet and a tranquil spirit, he marks out what especially belongs to women; for nothing becomes them more than a placid and a sedate temper of mind. For we know how outrageous a being is an imperious and a self-willed woman. And further, nothing is more fitted to correct the vanity of which Peter speaks than a placid quietness of spirit. What follows, that it is in the sight of God of great price, may be referred to the whole previous sentence as well as to the word spirit; the meaning indeed will remain the same. For why do women take so much care to adorn themselves, except that they may turn the eyes of men on themselves? But Peter, on the contrary, bids them to be more anxious for what is before God of a great price.[1]

Women's Clothing That Does Not "Hit the Golden Mean"

The aged women likewise, that they be in behaviour as becometh holiness, not false accusers, not given to much wine, teachers of good things. - Titus 2:3

We very frequently see, that females advanced in age either continue to dress with the lightness of youthful years, or have something superstitious in their apparel, and seldom hit the golden mean. Paul wished to guard against both extremes, by enjoining them to follow a course that is agreeable both to outward propriety and to religion; or, if you choose to express it in simpler language, to give evidence, by their very dress, that they are holy and godly women.

He next corrects another two vices, to which they are often addicted, when he forbids them to be slanderers and slaves to much wine. Talkativeness is a disease of women, and it is increased by old age. To this is added, that women never think that they are eloquent enough, if they are not given to prattling and to slander - if they do not attack the characters of all. The consequence is, that old women, by their slanderous talkativeness, as by a lighted torch, frequently set on fire many houses. Many are also given to drinking, so that, forgetting modesty and gravity, they indulge in an unbecoming wantonness.[2]

On Extravagance - the Servant's Gifts of Ornaments To Rebekah

And it came to pass, as the camels had done drinking, that the man took a golden earring of half a shekel weight, and two bracelets for her hands of ten shekels weight of gold. - Genesis 24:22

His adorning the damsel with precious ornaments is a token of his confidence. For since it is evident by many proofs that he was an honest and careful servant, he would not throw away without discretion the treasures of his master. He knows, therefore, that these gifts will not be ill-bestowed; or, at least, relying on the goodness of God, he gives them, in faith, as an earnest of future marriage.

But it may be asked, whether God approves ornaments of this kind, which pertain not so much to neatness as to pomp? I answer, that the things related in Scripture are not always proper to be imitated.

Whatever the Lord commands in general terms is to be accounted as an inflexible rule of conduct; but to rely on particular examples is not only dangerous, but even foolish and absurd. Now we know how highly displeasing to God is not only pomp and ambition in adorning the body, but all kind of luxury. In order to free the heart from inward cupidity, he condemns that immoderate and superfluous splendor, which contains within itself many allurements to vice...

With respect to the earrings and bracelets of Rebekah, as I do not doubt that they were those in use among the rich, so the uprightness of the age allowed them to be sparingly and frugally used; and yet I do not excuse the fault. This example, however, neither helps us, nor alleviates our guilt, if, by such means, we excite and continually inflame those depraved lusts which, even when all incentives are removed, it is excessively difficult to restrain. The women who desire to shine in gold, seek in Rebekah a pretext for their corruption.[3]

CHAPTER 21

CARE FOR WIDOWS

Before the Church Is Burdened with Them, Let Them Do Their Duty

C alvin correctly understood that widows should be cared for, first by the family and second, by the church. This is in sharp contrast to our modern understanding where the state is the provider for widows. Calvin's exegesis led him to enumerate the various criteria for widow support, including the primacy of the family, indicating that "before the Church is burdened with them, let them do their duty." He urged that it be determined that they are "really widows" according to the biblical requirements. Her faithfulness at home and church under the biblical requirements was paramount in the equation and he emphasized that "widows should be trained by domestic apprenticeship to the worship of God." However, he points out that in the early church, when a widow met the requirements, she was taken "under the protection of the Church."

CALVIN SPEAKS:

What Does It Mean to Honor Widows?

Honour widows that are widows indeed. But if any widow have children or nephews, let them learn first to shew piety at home, and to requite their parents: for that is good and acceptable before God. - I Timothy 5:3-4

"Honor widows that are really widows." *By the word honor he does not mean any expression of respect, but that special care of them which bishops took in the ancient Church; for widows were taken under the protection of the Church, that they might be supported out of the common funds. The meaning of this mode of expression is as if he had said, "For selecting widows that are to be taken under your care and that of the deacons, you ought to consider who they are that are really widows. What was their condition we shall afterwards explain more fully. But we must here attend to the reason why Paul does not admit any but those who are absolutely widows, and, at the same time, widows without children; for, in that condition, they dedicated themselves to the Church, that they might withdraw from all the private concerns of a family, and might lay aside every hindrance. Justly, therefore, does*

Paul forbid to receive the mothers of families, who are already bound by a charge of a different kind. When he calls them "really widows", he alludes to the Greek word χήρα, which is derived ἀπὸ τοῦ χηροῦσθαι, from a verb which signifies to be "deprived" or "destitute."

"If any widow." There are various ways of explaining this passage; and the ambiguity arises from this circumstance, that the latter clause may refer either to widows or to their children. Nor is this consistent with the verb (let them learn) being plural, while Paul spoke of a widow in the singular number; for a change of number is very customary in a general discourse, that is, when the writer speaks of a whole class, and not of an individual. They who think that it relates to widows, are of the opinion that the meaning is, "let them learn, by the pious government of their family, to repay to their successors the education that they received from their ancestors." This is the explanation given by Chrysostom and some others. But others think that it is more natural to interpret it as relating to children and grandchildren. Accordingly, in their opinion, the Apostle teaches that the mother or grandmother is the person towards whom they should exercise their piety; for nothing is more natural than (ἀντιπελαργία) the return of filial for parental affection; and it is very unreasonable that it should be excluded from the Church. Before the Church is burdened with them, let them do their duty.

Hereto I have related the opinion of others. But I wish my readers to consider if it would not agree better with the context in this manner: "Let them learn to conduct themselves in a godly manner at home." As if he had said, that it would be valuable as a preparatory instruction, that they should train themselves to the worship of God, by performing godly offices at home towards their relatives; for nature commands us to love our parents next to God; that this secondary piety leads to the highest piety. And as Paul saw that the very rights of nature were violated under the pretense of religion. In order to correct this fault, he commanded that widows should be trained by domestic apprenticeship to the worship of God.

"To shew piety towards their own house." *Almost all the commentators take the verb εὐσεβεῖν in an active sense, because it is followed by an accusative; but that is not a conclusive argument, for it is customary with the Greek authors to have a preposition understood. And this exposition agrees well with the context, that, by cultivating human piety, they should train themselves in the worship of God; lest a foolish and silly devotion should divest them of human feelings. Again, let widows learn to repay what they owe to their ancestors by educating their own offspring.*

For this is good and acceptable before God. Not to shew gratitude to our ancestors is universally acknowledged to be monstrous; for that is a lesson taught us by natural reason. And not only is this conviction natural to all, that affection towards our parents is the second degree of piety; but the very storks teach us gratitude by their example; and that is the etymology of the word ἀνιπελαργία. But Paul, not satisfied with this, declares that God hath sanctioned it; as if he had said, "There is no reason why anyone should think that it has its origin in the opinion of men; but God hath so ordained."[1]

Advice on Widowhood and Remarriage

I will therefore that the younger women marry, bear children, guide the house, give none occasion to the adversary to speak reproachfully. - I Timothy 5:14

I wish the younger (widows) to marry. Censorious men laugh at this injunction of the Apostle. "As if," say they, "it had been necessary to stimulate their excessively strong desire; for who does not know that almost all widows have naturally a wish to be married?" Superstitious men, on the other hand, would reckon that this doctrine concerning marriage is highly unsuitable to an Apostle of Christ. But, after a careful examination of the whole matter, men of sound judgment will acknowledge that Paul teaches nothing here but what is necessary and highly useful. For, on the one hand, there are many to whom widowhood gives the opportunity of greater licentiousness; and, on the other hand, there are always arising spirits speaking lies in hypocrisy, who make holiness to consist in celibacy, as if it were angelical perfection, and either totally condemn marriage, or despise it as if it savored of the pollution of the flesh. There are few either of men or women that consider their calling. How rarely do you find a man who willingly bears the burden of governing a wife! The reason is, that it is attended by innumerable vexations. How reluctantly does a woman submit to the yoke!

Consequently, when Paul bids the younger widows marry, he does not invite them to nuptial delights; and, when he bids them bear children, he does not exhort them to indulge lust; but, taking into account the weakness of the sex, and the slipperiness of the age, he exhorts them to chaste marriage, and, at the same time, to the endurance of those burdens which belong to holy marriage. And he does this, especially, in order that he may not be thought to have acted contemptuously in excluding them from the rank of widows; for he means, that their life will be not less acceptable to God than if they remained in widowhood. And, indeed, God pays no regard to the superstitious opinions of men, but values this obedience more highly than all things else, when we comply with our calling, instead of permitting ourselves to be carried along by the wish of our own heart.

Having heard that consolation, they have no reason to complain that injury is done to them, or to take it in that they are excluded from one kind of honor; for they learn that, in the married state, they are not less acceptable to God, because they obey his calling. When he speaks of bearing children, he includes, under a single word, all the annoyances that must be endured in bringing up children; in the same manner as, under the government of the house, he includes all that belongs to household management.

"To give no occasion to the adversary." *For, as the husband may be said to be the covering of the wife, so widowhood is liable to many unfavorable suspicions. And what purpose does it serve, to arm the enemies of the gospel with calumnies, without any necessity? But it is very difficult for a widow, in the flower of her age, to act with such caution that wicked men shall not find some pretext for slandering her; and, therefore, if they sincerely desire edification, let them, in order to shut the mouth of evil speakers, choose a way of life that is less liable to suspicion. Here, I suppose, the common adversaries of the gospel to be meant, rather than the private adversaries of any woman; for Paul speaks indefinitely.*[2]

CHAPTER 22

INFANT BAPTISM

How Unjust... To Drive Away Those Whom Christ Invites To Himself

After the example of Christ, Calvin had arms open wide to children. Even though the author of this book disagrees with Calvin on the matter of infant baptism, we must acknowledge that the heart of his baptismal theology was his high view of children and the important priority of bringing them up in the training and admonition of the Lord. For Calvin, excluding them from baptism was anathema in the face of Christ, who "by embracing them, he testified that they were reckoned by Christ among his flock." Baptismal theology and practice was the center of Calvin's theory of the family and its relationship with the church. Calvin believed that what happened at baptism collected up all the elements of family, church, and civil life, and established a trajectory for every child who would be initiated. Baptism marked the entry of children into the church and community. It was there that babies were named and the other mentors in the child's life were identified, establishing the various relationships that would figure into the child's life for the glory of God. Parents, pastors, congregations, town authorities, and godparents were all included in the picture. The rite of baptism guaranteed the nourishment of the spiritual sensibilities of a child from the cradle to the grave, and identified him with the church, the family, and the city in which he lived.

CALVIN SPEAKS:

Sacrilege - to Drive Cherished Children from the Fold

But Jesus said, Suffer little children, and forbid them not, to come unto me: for of such is the kingdom of heaven. - Matthew 19:14

He declares that he wishes to receive children; and at length, taking them in his arms, he not only embraces, but blesses them by the laying on of hands; from which we infer that his grace is extended even to those who are of that age. And no wonder; for since the whole race of

Adam is shut up under the sentence of death, all from the least even to the greatest must perish, except those who are rescued by the only Redeemer. To exclude from the grace of redemption those who are of that age would be too cruel; and therefore it is not without reason that we employ this passage as a shield against the Anabaptists. They refuse baptism to infants, because infants are incapable of understanding that mystery which is denoted by it. We, on the other hand, maintain that, since baptism is the pledge and figure of the forgiveness of sins, and likewise of adoption by God, it ought not to be denied to infants, whom God adopts and washes with the blood of his Son. Their objection, that repentance and newness of life are also denoted by it, is easily answered. Infants are renewed by the Spirit of God, according to the capacity of their age, till that power which was concealed within them grows by degrees, and becomes fully manifest at the proper time. Again, when they argue that there is no other way in which we are reconciled to God, and become heirs of adoption, than by faith, we admit this as to adults, but, with respect to infants, this passage demonstrates it to be false. Certainly, the laying on of hands was not a trifling or empty sign, and the prayers of Christ were not idly wasted in air. But he could not present the infants solemnly to God without giving them purity. And for what did he pray for them, but that they might be received into the number of the children of God? Hence it follows, that they were renewed by the Spirit to the hope of salvation. In short, by embracing them, he testified that they were reckoned by Christ among his flock. And if they were partakers of the spiritual gifts, which are represented by Baptism, it is unreasonable that they should be deprived of the outward sign. But it is presumption and sacrilege to drive far from the fold of Christ those whom he cherishes in his bosom, and to shut the door, and exclude as strangers those whom he does not wish to be forbidden to come to him.

For of such is the kingdom of heaven. Under this term he includes both little children and those who resemble them; for the Anabaptists foolishly exclude children, with whom the subject must have commenced; but at the same time, taking occasion from the present occurrence, he intended to exhort his disciples to lay aside malice and pride, and put on the nature of children. Accordingly, it is added by Mark and Luke, that no man can enter into the kingdom of heaven unless he be made to resemble a child.[1]

We Should Not Exclude Those Whom He Spontaneously Admits

Hence our Lord Jesus Christ, to give an example from which the world might learn that he had come to enlarge rather than to limit the grace of the Father, kindly takes the little children in his arms, and rebukes his disciples for attempting to prevent them from coming (Matt. 19:13), because they were keeping those to whom the kingdom of heaven belonged away from him, through whom alone there is access to heaven. But it will be asked, What resemblance is there between baptism and our Saviour embracing little children? He is not said to have baptised, but to have received, embraced, and blessed them; and, therefore, if we would imitate his example, we must give infants the benefit of our prayers, not baptise them. But let us attend to the act of our Saviour a little more carefully than these men do. For we must not lightly overlook the fact, that our Saviour, in ordering little children to be brought to him, adds the reason, "of such is the kingdom of heaven." And he afterwards testifies his good will by act, when he embraces them, and with prayer and benediction commends them to his Father. If it is right that children should be brought to Christ, why should they not be admitted to baptism, the symbol of our communion and fellowship with Christ? If the kingdom of heaven is theirs, why should they be denied the sign by which access, as it were, is opened to the Church, that being admitted into it they may be enrolled among the heirs of the heavenly kingdom? How unjust were we to drive away those whom Christ invites to himself, to spoil those whom he adorns with his gifts, to exclude those whom he spontaneously admits. But if we insist on discussing the difference between our Saviour's act and baptism, in how much higher esteem shall we hold baptism, (by which we testify that infants are included in the divine covenant), than the taking up,

*embracing, laying hands on children, and praying over
them, acts by which Christ, when present, declares both
that they are his, and are sanctified by him? By the other
cavils by which the objectors endeavour to evade this
passage, they only betray their ignorance: they quibble
that, because our Saviour says, "Suffer little children to
come," they must have been several years old, and fit to
come. But they are called by the Evangelists "brethe kai
paidia", terms which denote infants still at their mothers'
breasts. The term "come" is used simply for "approach."
See the quibbles to which men are obliged to have recourse
when they have hardened themselves against the truth!
There is nothing more solid in their allegation, that the
kingdom of heaven is not assigned to children, but to
those like children, since the expression is, "of such," not
"of themselves." If this is admitted, what will be the reason
which our Saviour employs to show that they are not
strangers to him from nonage? When he orders that little
children shall be allowed to come to him, nothing is plainer
than that mere infancy is meant. Lest this should seem
absurd, he adds, "Of such is the kingdom of heaven." But if
infants must necessarily be comprehended the expression,
"of such," clearly shows that infants themselves, and those
like them, are intended.*[2]

Omit Theatrical Pomp in Baptism

How much better it would be to omit from baptism all theatrical pomp, which dazzles the eyes of the simple and deadens their minds; whenever anyone is to be baptized, to present him to the assembly of believers and, with the whole church looking on as witness and praying over him, offer him to God; to recite the confession of faith with which the catechumen should be instructed; to recount the promises to be had in baptism; to baptize the catechumen in the name of the Father and of the Son and of the Holy Spirit (Matthew 28:19); lastly, to dismiss him with prayers and thanksgiving. If this were done, nothing essential would be omitted; and that one ceremony, which came from God, its author, not buried in outlandish pollutions, would shine in its full brightness.[3]

The Status of Children Who Die Before Their Baptism

But this controversy will at once be disposed of when we maintain, that children who happen to depart this life before an opportunity of immersing them in water, are not excluded from the kingdom of heaven. Now, it has been seen, that unless we admit this position, great injury is done to the covenant of God, as if in itself it were weak, whereas its effect depends not either on baptism, or on any accessaries. The sacrament is afterwards added as a kind of seal, not to give efficacy to the promise, as if in itself invalid, but merely to confirm it to us. Hence it follows, that the children of believers are not baptised, in order that though formerly aliens from the Church, they may then, for the first time, become children of God, but rather are received into the Church by a formal sign, because, in virtue of the promise, they previously belonged to the body of Christ. Hence if, in omitting the sign, there is neither sloth, nor contempt, nor negligence, we are safe from all danger. By far the better course, therefore, is to pay such respect to the ordinance of God as not to seek the sacraments in any other quarter than where the Lord has deposited them. When we cannot receive them from the Church, the grace of God is not so inseparably annexed to them that we cannot obtain it by faith, according to his word.[4]

CHAPTER 23

THE SANCTITY OF LIFE

It is a Monstrous Crime to Rob the Fetus of Life

The modern "pro-life" movement has a friend in John Calvin, for he railed against the destruction of life in the womb declaring it to be "an unforgivable crime." He called it "wickedness," "cruel," and "shameful." Calvin spares nothing in his diatribes against those who would murder a baby in the womb. His uncompromising position was that the "fetus, though enclosed in the womb of his mother, is already a human being, and it is a monstrous crime to rob it of life which it has not yet begun to enjoy." He viewed a baby in the womb as "part of the human race."

Calvin Speaks:

Abortion

If men strive, and hurt a woman with child, so that her fruit depart from her, and yet no mischief follow: he shall be surely punished, according as the woman's husband will lay upon him; and he shall pay as the judges determine. And if any mischief follow, then thou shalt give life for life. - Exodus 21:22-23

The fetus, though enclosed in the womb of his mother, is already a human being, and it is a monstrous crime to rob it of life which it has not yet begun to enjoy. If it seems more horrible to kill a man in his own house than in a field, because a man's house is his place of most secure refuge, it ought surely to be deemed more atrocious to destroy a fetus in the womb before it has come to light.[1]

Quenching the Hope of a Family

And Onan knew that the seed should not be his; and it came to pass, when he went in unto his brother's wife, that he spilled it on the ground, lest that he should give seed to his brother. And the thing which he did displeased the LORD: wherefore he slew him also. - Genesis 38:9-10

I will content myself with briefly mentioning this, as far as the sense of shame allows to discuss it. It is a horrible thing to pour out seed besides the intercourse of man and woman. Deliberately avoiding the intercourse, so that the seed drops on the ground, is doubly horrible. For this means that one quenches the hope of his family, and kills the son, which could be expected, before he is born. This wickedness is now as severely as is possible condemned by the Spirit, through Moses, that Onan, as it were, through a violent and untimely birth, tore away the seed of his brother out the womb, and as cruel as shamefully was thrown on the earth. Moreover he thus has, as much as was in his power, tried to destroy a part of the human race. When a woman in some way drives away the seed out the womb, through aids, then this is rightly seen as an unforgivable crime. Onan was guilty of a similar crime, by defiling the earth with his seed, so that Tamar would not receive a future inheritor.[2]

SECTION III

WHEN CALVIN GOT
IT WRONG

CHAPTER 24

LEARNING FROM IMPERFECT MEN

Understanding Heroes and Their Flaws

W e may not agree with Calvin on every point of theological principle or application of Scripture. While he was a very bright star and used of God to cause many things to be set in order, we must also acknowledge that he was a mere man looking through a glass darkly.

We may take exception with elements of Calvin's view of the church or his practice of posting guards at the baptismal font or his usurping of fathers' roles by not allowing them to name their children the way they desired. We may believe the Consistory was wrong on this or that ruling or even that it was unbiblical.

How do we process the things which we believe were wrong with Calvin and the reformers of Geneva? What do we do with

Calvin's flaws or blindness in certain areas? Let me propose four things we should remember when evaluating any personality, movement, or historical period.

Remember the Realities of Our Sanctification

Like every believer who has been rescued from perdition, the Reformers also needed reforming. We should acknowledge that no one is able to completely rise above a culture, knowing that personal sanctification comes more slowly than we or others would like. We are often blind and sinful and cannot see the logs in our own eyes.

Remember the Humanity of All Men

The battle is fierce in times of reformation and life moves fast enough that often things are missed in the normal pressures of life or in the crush of controversy and sickness. We ought to grant to the Reformers the same patience we would want for ourselves in the midst of difficult times.

Remember the Flaws of Our Fathers in the Faith

A quick recollection of the foibles of our dear fathers Abraham, David, Jonah, and Peter should temper our censure. Yes, they could have done better. They could have made better decisions. They could have avoided certain problems from our perspective. But they were justified by faith not works. There are no perfect men. But there are great men, like Calvin, who can teach us much, even though they did not have the perfections we might wish they did.

Remember to Ask Calvin's Question

What saith the Scriptures? Calvin always wanted to know what Scripture said. This is the most important focal point in responding to Calvin's ministry.

The best course of action in dealing with our dear brothers in the faith, with whom we may disagree, is to be prayerful and wise, taking the best from them, and then moving on rather than obsessing about whatever flaws we might find.

What we do know about Calvin is that he deeply desired to love the Word of God by obeying it and delighting in it. The inscription on his personal emblem tells the whole story,

"My heart I offer to you, O Lord, promptly and sincerely."

Calvin desired to be hemmed in by the Word of God - even at the risk of his reputation, his possessions, his family, and his very life. This is the beginning point of all reformation.

SECTION IV

THE REST OF THE STORY

CHAPTER 25

AN EFFECTIVE FAMILY REFORMATION

The Importance of the Next Generation

While it is true that Calvin never wrote a book on the family, the reformation started by his influence did not simply die out. It laid a foundation of terminology and principles that others would draw upon for centuries to come and it passed on the torch to the next generation. The doctrine survived, spreading across Europe and finally traveling to America with the pilgrim settlers in the early seventeenth century.

The successors to the Reformers - the Puritans - took the foundational principles of family life which Calvin expounded and built upon them, publishing volume after volume on the subject. Stephen Ozment comments that,

"[H]ome and family were no longer objects of widespread ridicule, a situation that lasted until modern times. The first generation of Protestant reformers died believing they had released women into the world by establishing them firmly at the center of home and family life, no longer to suffer the withdrawn, culturally circumscribed, sexually repressed, male regulated life of a cloister. And they believed children would never again be consigned at an early age to involuntary celibacy but would henceforth remain in the home, objects of constant parental love and wrath, until they were properly married." [1]

The basic reforms that sprung from this biblical vision of family life continued to be developed far beyond the sixteenth century. The Scripture teaches that the family was designed by God to be a spiritual training ground for children serving similar functions as the Church. Calvin clearly understood this, stating in his commentary on Genesis, "every family... ought to be a church."[2] This statement revolutionized the common understanding of family life. From Calvin on, this idea would appear in the writings of dozens of Puritan pastors and their successors including Richard Baxter, Phillip Dodderidge, Richard Mather, Jonathan Edwards, and Charles Spurgeon. In 1704, Matthew Henry even named one of his sermons "A Church in the House."

What About a Family Reformation Today?

In the same way that the family needed to be reformed according to Scripture in the Reformation era, family life in our day needs to be reformed. The disappearance of biblical family life in our world is astonishing. The root cause is the same as it was in the sixteenth century - the biblical order for church and family is lost because the sufficiency of Scripture is rejected.

In today's marriages, emotion trumps commitment, sexuality displaces love, compatibility compromises covenant, independence outweighs procreation, headship dies due to egalitarianism, and marriage ceremonies major on creativity and minor on biblical principle. Marriages dissolve at a faster rate in the "church" than outside of it. Husbands either neglect or dominate their wives. Wives do not submit to or respect their husbands. Fathers do not shepherd their families. Parents neglect their responsibilities to their children. Children are not catechized. Youth have no knowledge of biblical truth and cannot accurately explain important points of Bible doctrine. One generation despises the other. Babies are delayed, avoided, or aborted. A corrosive dating culture defiles the younger generation. There is no honor in the family and the home is turned into a flophouse instead of a household of faith and industry.

As it was in Geneva before the Reformation, today's family is a house of inventions. The structure and practice that Scripture advocates is nearly nonexistent. Today, families are more inventions of Hollywood than Holy Scripture.

CHAPTER 26

TWELVE SIGNS OF TODAY'S FAMILY REFORMATION

The Fruits of Obedience Observed

There is, however, a family reformation movement afoot today. The same principle that transformed the family in Geneva is bringing about family reformation in our own time.

This reformation, which is springing up among many whose hearts are being offered to the Lord, has at its heart a desire to obey Scripture in matters of family life. The following are a number of signs of this family reformation.

1. Revival of Biblical Fatherhood

Droves of fathers have turned their hearts toward home. The results can be seen in a renewed interest and emphasis on family worship, a recognition that the family is the center of discipleship, and an acknowledgment that the father is the primary provider of instruction. The home education movement, with its roots in the biblical doctrine of education and the proper role of fathers in discipleship, reflects this aspect of family renewal.

2. Large Families

High fertility rates are on the rise in the home education movement. This can be proven simply by counting the fifteen passenger vans at the homeschool conferences. In the church I attend, the average family size is 7 and the average number of children per woman is 5.2 while the national average is 2.05.[1] This is reflective of a reformation of attitudes toward children. Homeschool families are having many children and thousands of men nationwide are having vasectomy reversals in order to obey Scripture on the issue of fertility.

3. Rejection of Feminism

The traditional feminist career track is being challenged and overthrown as daughters in thousands of families in America are understanding and being reformed by the biblical vision of womanhood. They are staying home and promoting the prosperity of their families by helping their mothers raise children and making the home a place of industry and spiritual awakening.

4. Modest Dress

Women are developing a new awareness of the importance of biblical modesty and the implications of the gospel for their apparel. In the past decade, dozens of books have been released which deal with the subject using the words of Scripture as the main argument.

5. Early Manhood

I am observing a rising number of young men who have determined to reject frivolity, lust, and idleness, preferring the biblical pattern of discipleship and sobriety. Some are even becoming providers and fathers at an early age instead of spending the years of their youth with games and sports of little value in establishing a foundation for marriage and family.

6. Persecution

People have been rejected by their families and sometimes even from their churches for trying to be faithful to the Word of God. Many have suffered exclusion and censure simply because they rejected the current socially accepted patterns of family life.

7. Generational Retention

The loss of the next generation to Christianity seems to be slowed down in circles where family reformation is occurring. While the astonishing loss of 70-90% of the next generation continues in those established churches which prefer to continue the modern, unbiblical patterns of age segregation, the opposite statistic can be found in churches which seek to honor biblical patterns and to reform their families.

8. Books on Family Life

There is an outpouring of new books of family life that have their basis in Scripture. Instead of books that focus on psychology and the latest marketplace success techniques, there are a rising number of books being written where the authors are satisfied to focus exclusively on key biblical texts that explain family life.

9. Resurgence of Expository Preaching

As in Calvin's Geneva, there is a modern resurgence of the practice of "expository preaching." This practice, once it is embraced, stimulates conformity to biblical practices and values for family life.

10. Clarification of the Gospel

Genuine family reformation hinges on a right understanding of the gospel, for without it, the rising generation can easily be duped into believing they are Christians because of false views of works or repentance. There is a revival in the understanding of the gospel, with new organizations being created to promote the preaching of the true gospel.

11. Doctrinal Awareness

It has become quite well known that there is a revival of Calvinistic/Reformed theology in twenty-first century America. A companion to this is a renewed awareness of the doctrine of the sufficiency of Scripture. This awareness is awakening many people in the church to the fact that they have not been carefully applying the Word of God to every area of life – including family life.

12. Family Integrated Church Movement

Over the past decade, there has been significant upheaval in established churches over questions regarding age segregated church life, the methods and philosophy of modern youth ministry, and the distinctive roles of fathers and mothers in the church. This is coupled with a wave of church planting which features many of the above signs of awakening incorporated into everyday church life. This methodology of family integration rejects the age segregated and feministic church models of the last half century as modern inventions.

These twelve signs are markers of a spiritual awakening and they are occurring as a result of a desire to know and do the will of God. Each of the above elements represents a point of obedience to Scripture arising from a desire to be conformed to divine patterns and to obey the Word of the Lord in all matters of life – including family life.

CHAPTER 27

HOPE FOR THE FUTURE

Calvin's Spiritual Grandchildren

The family was reformed by the simple exposition of Scripture in Calvin's Geneva. The reformation needed today will only occur as local church pastors preach the Word, give the whole counsel of God through faithful exposition of Scripture, identify critical texts for family life, and fearlessly apply that teaching - much like John Calvin in Geneva. When they do, they should expect not only the fruits of righteousness, but also the tumults and fights that come when one treads on the ground defiled by the serpent.

Consider Calvin's spiritual offspring. As parents taught their children the simple biblical truths of the reformation, a generational legacy was established that continues even to this day. There are many stories of Protestant martyrs whose children were so infused with the truths of Scripture by their parents, that they too became martyrs. Consider Calvin's "Sola Scriptura" legacy one hundred years later in the lives of two Covenanter girls who were martyred in the "killing times" - Marion Harvie (20) and Isabel Alison (13). These young ladies were tried together on one indictment and executed the same day on January 26, 1681. While they were on the gallows, they sang Psalm 23 and Psalm 84. They glorified God that day, and praised Him to their last breath. Notice the maturity and passion of these two daughters of Zion. Marion wrote,

> Now, farewell holy and sweet Scriptures, which were aye my comfort in the midst of all my difficulties. Farewell faith, farewell hope, farewell wanderers, who have been comfortable to my soul, in the hearing of them commend Christ's love. Farewell brethren, farewell, sisters; farewell Christian acquaintances; farewell, sun, moon, and stars! And now, welcome my lovely and heartsome Christ Jesus, into whose hands I commit my spirit through all eternity.[1]

Isabel wrote,

> But what shall I say to the commendation of Christ and His Cross? I bless the Lord, praise to His holy name, that hath made my prison a palace to me.[2]

Pastor Alexander Peden said of Isabel and Marion, "They were two honest worthy lassies." These were the spiritual granddaughters of John Calvin.

This was the legacy of *sola Scriptura*. May God give us many such sons and daughters who love Scripture, more than life itself.

END NOTES

SECTION I

CHAPTER 1

1. Witte, John Jr., and Kingdon, Robert M., *Sex, Marriage, and Family in John Calvin's Geneva: Courtship, Engagement, and Marriage.*, edited by Browning, Don and Witte, John Jr. (Grand Rapids, MI: Eerdmans Publishing Company, 2005), 74.

2. *The Registers of the Consistory of Geneva in the Time of Calvin*, Vol. 1, trans. M. Wallace McDonald, edited by Robert M. Kingdon, Thomas A. Lambert, and Isabella M. Watt (Grand Rapids, MI: William B. Eerdmans Publishing Company), XI.

3. Calvin, John, Commentary on Genesis, Vol. 1, trans. John King (Grand Rapids, MI: Baker Books, reprinted 2003), 481.

CHAPTER 2

1. Calvin, John, *Institutes of the Christian Religion* (Bellingham, WA: Logos Research Systems, Inc., 1997), S. IV, xix, 33.

2. *Ibid.*, S. IV, xv, 19.

3. *Ibid.*, S. IV, xix, 33.

4. *Ibid.*, S. I, vii, 5.

5. Knox, John, *The Works of John Knox*, Vol. 3, "A Vindication of the Doctrine that the Sacrifice of the Mass is Idolatry," collected and edited by David Laing (Edinburgh, Scotland: 1854), 29-70.

CHAPTER 3

1. Parker, T.H.L., *Calvin's Preaching* (Edinburgh, Scotland: T&T Clark, 1992), 6-7.

2. *Ibid.*, 7.

3. Calvin, John, *Institutes of the Christian Religion,* trans. Henry Beveridge (ebook, Ages Bible Software 1998), S. I, xiv, 1.

4. Genesis 2:18, 22-24; 3:16; 4:7, 19; 5:2; 6:1-4; 12:2-3; 17, 17:7; 18:19; 20:3-18; 21:7; 24:2-5, 22; 29:18; 33:5; 34:4; 38:9-10; 39:6 ... Exodus 2:1-3; 10:2; 20:12, 14; 21:17, 22-23 ... Leviticus 18:6; 20:9 ... Deuteronomy 5:9; 21:11-12; 22:13, 23 ... Numbers 14:18 ... Joshua 15:16-17 ... Psalms 78:4, 127:3-5 ... Proverbs 2:17; 12:4; 20:7, 20; 21:18-21; 24:1 ... Isaiah 39:7 ... Jeremiah 32:18 ... Malachi 2:14-16; 4:6 ... Matthew 5:4-6, 27-28, 31; 19: 3-6, 13-14 ... Luke 1:25 ... John 2:1-2 ... Romans 13:14 ... I Corinthians 7:1, 34; 9:5; 11:7-8; 14:34-35 ... II Corinthians 6:14 ... Ephesians 5:23, 25, 28-29, 31-32; 6:1-4 ... Colossians 3:18-20 ... 1 Thessalonians 4:5 ... I Timothy 2:11-12; 3:4-5; 4:1, 3; 5:1, 3-4 ... Titus 1:6; 2:3-5 ... Hebrews 13:4 ... I Peter 3:1-4

5. Lawson, Steven, *The Expository Genius of John Calvin* (Lake Mary, FL: Reformation Trust Publishing, 2007), 71.

6. Calvin, John, *Commentary on Genesis,* Vol. 1, trans. John King (Grand Rapids, MI: Baker Books, reprinted 2003), 128-129.

7. Calvin, John, *Commentary on Genesis,* Vol. 1, trans. John King (Grand Rapids, MI: Baker Books, reprinted 2003), 136.

8. *Ibid.*

9. Calvin, John, *Harmony of the Law,* Vol. 3, trans. Charles Bingham (Grand Rapids, MI: Baker Books, reprinted 2003), 7-9.

10. Calvin, John, *Harmony of the Law,* Vol. 3, trans. Charles Bingham (Grand Rapids, MI: Baker Books, reprinted 2003), 13-14.

11. Ozment, Steve, *When Fathers Ruled: Family Life in Reformation Europe* (Cambridge, MA: Harvard University Press, 1985), 9.

12. Good, James, *Famous Women of the Reformed Church* (Birmingham, AL: Solid Ground Publishing), 24.

13. *Ibid.*, 26-27.

14. Schaff, Phillip, *History of the Christian Church* (New York: Charles Scribner's Sons, 1888), 461.

CHAPTER 4

1.   Naphy, William G., *"Baptism, Church Riots, and Social Unrest in Calvin's Geneva," Sixteenth Century Journal*, vol. 226, no.1 (1995), 92.

2.   *Ibid.*, 95.

CHAPTER 5

1.   Ozment, Steve, *When Fathers Ruled: Family Life in Reformation Europe* (Cambridge, MA: Harvard University Press, 1985), 1.

2.   *Ibid.*, 2.

3.   Tucker, Ruth & Liefeld, Walter, *Daughters of the Church* (Grand Rapids, MI: Zondervan Publishing House, 1987), 175.

4.   *Ibid.*, 197.

5.   *Ibid.*, 179.

6.   *Ibid.*, 180.

7.   Witte, John Jr., and Kingdon, Robert M., *Sex, Marriage, and Family in John Calvin's Geneva: Courtship, Engagement, and Marriage.*, edited by Browning, Don and Witte, John Jr. (Grand Rapids, MI: Eerdmans Publishing Company, 2005), 1.

8.   Calvin, John, *Institutes of the Christian Religion* (Bellingham, WA : Logos Research Systems, Inc., 1997), IV, xvi, 7.

9.   Spierling, Karen E., *Infant Baptism in Reformation Geneva* (Burlington, VT: Ashgate Publishing, 2005), 65.

10. *Ibid.*, 55.

11. See Appendix B.

12. Spierling, Karen E., *Infant Baptism in Reformation Geneva* (Burlington, VT: Ashgate Publishing, 2005), 200.

13. Piper, John & Taylor, Justin, *Sex and the Supremacy of Christ* (Wheaton, IL: Crossway Books, 2005), 247-248. Original source: Bailey, Derek, Sexual Relations in Christian Thought (New York: Harper & Brothers, 1959), 133, n.3, cited in Daniel Doriani, "The Puritans, Sex, and Pleasure," Westminster Theological Journal 53 (Spring 1991): 142 [125-143].

14. Witte, John Jr., and Kingdon, Robert M., *Sex, Marriage, and Family in John Calvin's Geneva: Courtship, Engagement, and Marriage.*,

edited by Browning, Don and Witte, John Jr. (Grand Rapids, MI: Eerdmans Publishing Company, 2005), 481.

SECTION II

CHAPTER 6

1.   Calvin, John: *Institutes of the Christian Religion* (Bellingham, WA: Logos Research Systems, Inc., 1997), S. II, viii, 21.
2.   Calvin, John, *Tracts and Letters,* Vol. 4, Letter #25, ed. by Henry Beveridge & Jules Bonnet (ebook, Ages Bible Software, 1998), 88.
3.   Calvin, John, *Harmony of the Law,* Vol. 2, trans. by Charles Bingham (Grand Rapids, MI: Baker Books, reprinted 2003), 75.
4.   Calvin, John: *Institutes of the Christian Religion* (Bellingham, WA: Logos Research Systems, Inc., 1997), S. II, viii, 19, 20.

CHAPTER 7

1.   Witte, John Jr., and Kingdon, Robert M., *Sex, Marriage, and Family in John Calvin's Geneva: Courtship, Engagement, and Marriage..* Edited by Browning, Don and Witte, John Jr. (Grand Rapids, MI: Eerdmans Publishing Company, 2005), 10.
2.   Calvin, John, *Commentary on Genesis*, Vol. 1, trans. John King (Grand Rapids, MI: Baker Books, reprinted 2003), 134.
3.   *Ibid.,* 128-129.
4.   *Ibid.,* 136.
5.   *Ibid.,* 136-137.
6.   *Ibid.,* 228.
7.   Calvin, John, *Commentary on Twelve Minor Prophets*, Vol. 5, trans. John Owen (Grand Rapids, MI: Baker Books, reprinted 2003), 553.
8.   Calvin, John, *Commentary on Genesis,* Vol. 1, trans. John King (Grand Rapids, MI: Baker Books, reprinted 2003), 130.

9. Calvin, John, *Commentary on Galatians and Ephesians,* trans. William Pringle (Grand Rapids, MI: Baker Books, reprinted 2003), 322-323.

10. Calvin, John, *Institutes of the Christian Religion,* trans. Henry Beveridge (eBook, Ages Bible Software 1998), S. IV, xii, 24.

11. Calvin, John, *Commentary on the Gospel of John,* trans. John King (eBook, Ages Bible Software, 1998), 68-73.

12. Calvin, John, *Institutes of the Christian Religion,* trans. Henry Beveridge (eBook, Ages Bible Software 1998), S. IV, xii, 25.

13. *Ibid.,* S. IV, ix, 14.

14. *Ibid.,* S. IV, xix, 34-37.

15. *Ibid.,* S. IV, xiii, 21.

16. *Ibid.,* S. IV, xii, 23.

CHAPTER 8

1. Calvin, John, Commentary on Galatians and Ephesians, trans. William Pringle (Grand Rapids, MI: Baker Books, reprinted 2003), 318-319.

2. Calvin, John, Institutes of the Christian Religion, trans. Henry Beveridge (eBook, Ages Bible Software 1998), S. IV, xix, 35.

3. Calvin, John, Commentary on Galatians and Ephesians, trans. William Pringle (Grand Rapids, MI: Baker Books, reprinted 2003), 318.

4. Calvin, John, Commentary on the Corinthians, Vol. 1, trans. William Pringle (Grand Rapids, MI: Baker Books, reprinted 2003), 357-358.

5. Calvin, John, Commentary on Galatians and Ephesians, trans. William Pringle (Grand Rapids, MI: Baker Books, reprinted 2003), 318.

6. Calvin, John, Sermons on Genesis, trans. John Field (ebook, Ages Bible Software, Old Paths Publications, 1996), 128.

7. Calvin, John, Commentary on Galatians and Ephesians, trans. William Pringle (Grand Rapids, MI: Baker Books, reprinted 2003), 322.

8. Calvin, John, Commentary on Philippians, Colossians and Thessalonians, trans. William Pringle (Grand Rapids, MI: Baker

Books, reprinted 2003), 219.

9.   Calvin, John, Commentary on Galatians and Ephesians, trans.
     William Pringle (Grand Rapids, MI: Baker Books, reprinted 2003),
     323.

CHAPTER 9

1.   Calvin, John, *Commentary on the Corinthians,* Vol. 1, trans. William
     Pringle (Grand Rapids, MI: Baker Books, reprinted 2003), 357.

2.   Calvin, John, *Commentary on Genesis,* Vol. 1, trans. John King
     (Grand Rapids, MI: Baker Books, reprinted 2003), 130-131.

3.   Calvin, John, *Commentary Twelve Minor Prophets,* Vol. 5, trans. John
     Owen (Grand Rapids, MI: Baker Books, reprinted 2003), 554.

4.   Calvin, John, *Tracts and Letters,* Vol. 5, Letter #238, edited by Henry
     Beveridge & Jules Bonnet (ebook, Ages Bible Software, 1998), 228

5.   Calvin, John, *Commentary on Genesis,* Vol. 1, trans. John King
     (Grand Rapids, MI: Baker Books, reprinted 2003), 129.

6.   Calvin, John, *Commentary on Galatians and Ephesians,* trans.
     William Pringle (Grand Rapids, MI: Baker Books, reprinted 2003),
     317.

7.   Calvin, John, *Commentary on Genesis,* Vol. 1, trans. John King
     (Grand Rapids, MI: Baker Books, reprinted 2003), 172.

8.   Calvin, John, *Tracts and Letters,* Vol. 4, Letter #111, edited by Henry
     Beveridge & Jules Bonnet (ebook, Ages Bible Software, 1998), 389.

9.   Calvin, John, *Tracts and Letters,* Vol. 5, Letter #146, edited by Henry
     Beveridge & Jules Bonnet (ebook, Ages Bible Software, 1998), 23.

10. Calvin, John, *Tracts and Letters,* Vol. 6, Letter #513, edited by Henry
     Beveridge & Jules Bonnet (ebook, Ages Bible Software, 1998), 460.

11. Calvin, John, *Commentary on The Catholic Epistles,* trans. John
     Owen (Grand Rapids, MI: Baker Books, reprinted 2003), 95-96.

12. Calvin, John, *Tracts and Letters,* Vol. 7, Letter #548, edited by Henry
     Beveridge & Jules Bonnet (ebook, Ages Bible Software, 1998), 79.

13. Calvin, John, *Institutes of the Christian Religion,* trans. Henry
     Beveridge (eBook, Ages Bible Software 1998), S. IV, xx, 29.

CHAPTER 10

1. Calvin, John, *Harmony of the Law,* Vol. 3, trans. Charles Bingham (Grand Rapids, MI: Baker Books, reprinted 2003), 68-69.

2. Calvin, John, Institutes of the Christian Religion, trans. Henry Beveridge (eBook, Ages Bible Software 1998), S. II, viii, 41.

3. Ibid., II.

4. Calvin, John, Harmony of the Gospels, Vol. 1, trans. William Pringle (Grand Rapids, MI: Baker Books, reprinted 2003), 290.

5. Calvin, John, Institutes of the Christian Religion, trans. Henry Beveridge (eBook, Ages Bible Software 1998), S. II, viii, 7, 49.

6. Calvin, John, Commentary on Genesis, Vol. 3, trans. John King (Grand Rapids, MI: Baker Books, reprinted 2003), 247.

7. Calvin, John, Commentary on Genesis, Vol. 1, trans. John King (Grand Rapids, MI: Baker Books, reprinted 2003), 523.

8. Calvin, John, Commentary on the First Epistle to the Thessalonians (eBook, Ages Bible Software, 1998), 639.

9. Calvin, John, Commentary Twelve Minor Prophets, Vol. 5, trans. John Owen (Grand Rapids, MI: Baker Books, reprinted 2003), 553.

10. Calvin, John, Commentary on Genesis, edited by John King (eBook, Ages Bible Software, 1998), 582.

11. Calvin, John, Harmony of the Law, Vol. 2, trans. Charles Bingham (Grand Rapids, MI: Baker Books, reprinted 2003), 93-94.

12. Calvin, John, Commentary Twelve Minor Prophets, Vol. 5, trans. John Owen (Grand Rapids, MI: Baker Books, reprinted 2003), 560.

13. Calvin, John, Harmony of the Gospels, Vol. 2, trans. William Pringle (Grand Rapids, MI: Baker Books, reprinted 2003), 377-379.

14. Calvin, John, Institutes of the Christian Religion, trans. Henry Beveridge (eBook, Ages Bible Software 1998), S. IV, i, 5.

15. Calvin, John, Commentary on Genesis, edited by John King (eBook, Ages Bible Software, 1998), 138.

CHAPTER 11

1. Calvin, John, Tracts and Letters, Vol. 6, Letter #368, edited by Henry Beveridge & Jules Bonnet (ebook, Ages Bible Software,

1998), 88.

2.	Calvin, John, Commentary on Genesis, Vol. 2, trans. John King (Grand Rapids, MI: Baker Books, reprinted 2003), 208.

3.	Calvin, John, Tracts and Letters Volume 6, Letter #389, edited by Henry Beveridge & Jules Bonnet (ebook, Ages Bible Software, 1998), 144.

4.	Calvin, John, Commentary on Psalms, Vol. 5, trans. James Anderson (Grand Rapids, MI: Baker Books, reprinted 2003), 110-112.

5.	Ibid.,111.

6.	Ibid., 112.

7.	Calvin, John, Harmony of the Gospels, Vol. 1, trans. William Pringle (Grand Rapids, MI: Baker Books, reprinted 2003), 30.

8.	Calvin, John, Commentary on Timothy, Titus, and Philemon, trans. William Pringle (Grand Rapids, MI: Baker Books, reprinted 2003), 70-71.

CHAPTER 12

1.	Calvin, John, Institutes of the Christian Religion (Bellingham, WA: Logos Research Systems, Inc., 1997), S. II, i, 7.

2.	Ibid., S. II, i, 8.

CHAPTER 13

1.	Calvin, John, Commentary Twelve Minor Prophets Volume 5, trans. John Owen (Grand Rapids, MI: Baker Books, reprinted 2003), 630.

2.	Calvin, John, Tracts and Letters Volume 5, Letter #332, edited by Henry Beveridge and Jules Bonnet (ebook, Ages Bible Software, 1998), 437.

3.	Calvin, John, Commentary on Genesis, Vol. 1, trans. John King (Grand Rapids, MI: Baker Books, reprinted 2003), 481.

4.	Calvin, John, Harmony of the Law, Vol. 1, trans. Charles Bingham (Grand Rapids, MI: Baker Books, reprinted 2003), 146.

5.	Calvin, John, Commentary on Psalms, Vol. 3, trans. James Anderson

(Grand Rapids, MI: Baker Books, reprinted 2003), 230.

CHAPTER 14

1. Calvin, John, Tracts and Letters Volume 5, Letter #229, edited by Henry Beveridge and Jules Bonnet (ebook, Ages Bible Software, 1998), 203.
2. Calvin, John, Institutes of the Christian Religion (Bellingham, WA: Logos Research Systems, Inc., 1997), S. IV, xix, 13.

CHAPTER 15

1. Calvin, John, *Sermons on Genesis*, trans. John Field (ebook, ages Bible Software, 1996), 180.
2. Calvin, John, *Commentary on Galatians and Ephesians*, trans. William Pringle (Grand Rapids, MI: Baker Books, reprinted 2003), 328-329.
3. Calvin, John, *Tracts and Letters* Volume 6, Letter #343, edited by Henry Beveridge and Jules Bonnet (ebook, Ages Bible Software, 1998), 26.

CHAPTER 16

1. Calvin, John, *Institutes of the Christian Religion* (Bellingham, WA: Logos Research Systems, Inc., 1997), S. III, xx, 37.
2. Calvin, John, *Harmony of the Gospels*, Vol. 2, edited by Charles Bingham (eBook, Ages Bible Software, 1998), 256-259.

Chapter 17

1. Calvin, John, *Harmony of the Law*, Vol. 3, trans. Charles Bingham (Grand Rapids, MI: Baker Books, reprinted 2003), 7-9.
2. Calvin, John, *Commentary on Galatians and Ephesians*, trans. William Pringle (Grand Rapids, MI: Baker Books, reprinted 2003), 326-329.
3. Calvin, John, *Institutes of the Christian Religion* (Bellingham, WA: Logos Research Systems, Inc., 1997), S. II, viii, 35-37.
4. Calvin, John, *Commentary on Philippians, Colossians and Thessalonians*, trans. William Pringle (Grand Rapids, MI: Baker Books, reprinted 2003), 219-220.
5. Calvin, John, *Commentary on Galatians and Ephesians*, trans. William Pringle (Grand Rapids, MI: Baker Books, reprinted 2003), 326-329.
6. Calvin, John, *Institutes of the Christian Religion* (Bellingham, WA: Logos Research Systems, Inc., 1997), S. II, viii, 35.
7. *Ibid.*, S. II, viii, 36.
8. *Ibid*, S. II, viii, 38.
9. Calvin, John, *Harmony of the Law*, Vol. 3, trans. Charles Bingham (Grand Rapids, MI: Baker Books, reprinted 2003), 13-14.
10. Calvin, John: *Institutes of the Christian Religion* (Bellingham, WA: Logos Research Systems, Inc., 1997), S. IV, xx, 29.

Chapter 18

1. Calvin, John, *Commentary on the Corinthians*, Vol. 1, trans. William Pringle (Grand Rapids, MI: Baker Books, reprinted 2003), 222-223.
2. *Ibid.*, 223-224.
3. Calvin, John, *Commentary on Genesis*, trans. John King (eBook, Ages Bible Software, 1998), 427-428.
4. Calvin, John, *Commentary on the Corinthians*, Vol. 2, trans. William Pringle (Grand Rapids, MI: Baker Books, reprinted 2003), 257-258.
5. Calvin, John, *Harmony of the Law*, Vol. 2, edited by the Rev. Charles

William Bingham (eBook, Ages Bible Software, 1998), 251-252.

6. Calvin, John, *Commentary on Malachi*, trans. John Owen (eBook, Ages Bible Software, 1998), 81-82.

7. Calvin, John, *Commentary on Genesis*, Vol. 2, trans. John King (Grand Rapids, MI: Baker Books, reprinted 2003), 130.

8. *Ibid.*

9. Calvin, John, *Commentary on Genesis*, Vol.1, trans. John King (Grand Rapids, MI: Baker Books, reprinted 2003), 154-155.

10. Calvin, John, *Harmony of the Law*, Vol. 3, trans. Charles Bingham (Grand Rapids, MI: Baker Books, reprinted 2003), 212.

11. Calvin, John, *Tracts and Letters*, Vol. 4, Letter #44, edited by Henry Beveridge and Jules Bonnet (ebook, Ages Bible Software, 1998), 168.

12. Calvin, John, *Commentary on Joshua*, trans. Henry Beveridge (Grand Rapids, MI: Baker Books, reprinted 2003), 93-94.

13. Witte, John Jr., and Kingdon, Robert M., *Sex, Marriage, and Family in John Calvin's Geneva: Courtship, Engagement, and Marriage..* Edited by Browning, Don and Witte, John Jr (Grand Rapids MI: Eerdmans Publishing Company, 2005), 44. Original source, Calvin, John, sermon on Deut 22:25-30.

14. Calvin, John, *Harmony of the Law*, Vol. 3, trans. Charles Bingham (eBook, Ages Bible Software, 1998), 63.

15. Calvin, John. *Harmony of the Law*, Vol. 2, trans. Charles Bingham (eBook, Ages Bible Software, 1998), 278-279.

16. Calvin, John, *Harmony of the Law*, Vol. 4, trans. Charles Bingham (Grand Rapids, MI: Baker Books, reprinted 2003), 101.

17. Calvin, John, *Harmony of the Law*, Vol. 3, trans. Charles Bingham (eBook, Ages Bible Software, 1998), 72.

18. Witte, John Jr., and Kingdon, Robert M., *Sex, Marriage, and Family in John Calvin's Geneva: Courtship, Engagement, and Marriage..* Edited by Browning, Don and Witte, John Jr. (Grand Rapids, MI: Eerdmans Publishing Company, 2005), 44. Original source, Calvin, John, Consilium, translated in Calvin's Ecclesiastical Advice, 122-123.

19. Calvin, John, *Commentary on Genesis*, trans. John King (eBook, Ages Bible Software, 1998), 429.

20. Calvin, John, *Harmony of the Law*, Vol. 4, trans. Charles Bingham (Grand Rapids, MI: Baker Books, reprinted 2003), 31.

21. Witte, John Jr., and Kingdon, Robert M., *Sex, Marriage, and Family*

in *John Calvin's Geneva: Courtship, Engagement, and Marriage.*.
Edited by Browning, Don and Witte, John Jr. (Grand Rapids, MI:
Eerdmans Publishing Company, 2005), 142-143. Original source,
Calvin, John, Consilium, translated in Calvin's Ecclesiastical Advice,
129-131.

Chapter 19

1. Calvin, John, *Commentary on Timothy, Titus, and Philemon*, trans.
    William Pringle (Grand Rapids, MI: Baker Books, reprinted 2003),
    119.
2. *Ibid.*
3. *Ibid.*, 291.
4. *Ibid.*, 291-292.
5. *Ibid.*, 82-83.
6. Calvin, John, *Commentary on the Corinthians*, Vol. 1, trans. William
    Pringle (Grand Rapids, MI: Baker Books, reprinted 2003), 468-
    469.
7. *Ibid.*
8. Calvin, John, *Commentary on Timothy, Titus, and Philemon*, trans.
    William Pringle (Grand Rapids, MI: Baker Books, reprinted 2003),
    67.
9. *Ibid.*, 312-313.

Chapter 20

1. Calvin, John, *Commentary on the Catholic Epistles*, trans. John Owen
    (Grand Rapids, MI: Baker Books, reprinted 2003), 96-97.
2. Calvin, John, *Commentary on Timothy, Titus, and Philemon*, trans.
    William Pringle (Grand Rapids, MI: Baker Books, reprinted 2003),
    311.
3. Calvin, John, *Commentary on Genesis*, trans. John King (eBook,
    Ages Bible Software, 1998), 435-436.

Chapter 21

1. Calvin, John, *Commentary on Timothy, Titus, and Philemon*, trans. William Pringle (Grand Rapids, MI: Baker Books, reprinted 2003), 120-121.

2. *Ibid.*, 134-135.

Chapter 22

1. Calvin, John, *Harmony of the Gospels*, Vol. 2, trans. William Pringle (Grand Rapids, MI: Baker Books, reprinted 2003), 390,391.

2. Calvin, John, *Institutes of the Christian Religion* (Bellingham, WA: Logos Research Systems, Inc., 1997), S. IV, xvi, 7.

3. *Ibid.*, S. IV, xv, 19.

4. *Ibid.*, S. IV, xv, 22.

Chapter 23

1. Calvin, John, *Harmony of the Law*, Vol. 3, trans. Charles Bingham (Grand Rapids, MI: Baker Books, reprinted 2003), 41, 42.

2. Calvin, John, *Commentary on Genesis*, Vol. 2, trans. John King (Grand Rapids, MI: Baker Books, reprinted 2003), 281.

Section VI

Chapter 25

1. Ozment, Steve, *When Fathers Ruled: Family Life in Reformation Europe* (Cambridge, MA: Harvard University Press, 1985), 49.

2. Calvin, John, *Commentary on Genesis*, trans. John King (ebook, Ages Bible Software, 1998), 319.

CHAPTER 26

1. "Total fertility rate: 2.05 children born/woman" (2009 est.) (*CIA World Factbook: https://www.cia.gov/library/publications/the-world-factbook/geos/us.html*)

CHAPTER 27

1. *Cloud of Witnesses*, reprinted by Rev. John Thompson (Harrisonburg, Va.: Sprinkle Publications, 1989), 144.
2. *Ibid.*, 129.